FOR PLAY

150 Sex Games
for Couples

Walter A. Shelburne

Illustrated by Molly Kiely

Waterfall Press
Oakland, California

FOR PLAY
150 Sex Games
for Couples

Illustrated by Molly Kiely

Cover design by Molly Kiely and Wei Lan Au

Published by Waterfall Press
5337 College Avenue, Suite 139
Oakland, California 94618

Library of Congress
Catalog Card Number 93-94059

ISBN 0-9636943-0-8

Printed in the United States of America

ACKNOWLEDGMENTS

I would like to acknowledge the help and support of several people who read my manuscript and gave me valuable feedback and critical support. Thanks to Paul Baclaski, Joanie Blank, John and Gail Craven, Jenise and Aribert Dormann, Frank Jur, Kumar, Kim Laurey, Donna Logsdon, Carolyn Mata, Jonathan Meyers, Peter Rengel, Tedde Rinker, Kathryn Roberts, Sarah Sand, Bob Tourkow, and Sue Wong.

Jay Wiseman is someone to whom I owe a special thanks for his moral support and technical advice.

Kathryn Roberts of the National Sexuality Symposium has also rendered invaluable aid, encouragement, and logistical support to this project.

Thanks are owed to Richard Shapiro for much patient graphic consultation and Rich Wingerter for computer help.

I thank Jim Chase and Elizabeth Powers for the generous contribution of their time and proofreading skills.

A special thank you for Don Spencer whose Erotic Massage Workshop was one of the original inspirations for this book.

I would also like to thank my illustrator, Molly Kiely, for capturing the spirit of the games.

DEDICATION

This book is dedicated to the little boy and the little girl in each of us.

WARNING AND DISCLAIMER

CONTENTS

LIST OF ILLUSTRATIONS

FOR PLAY
150 Sex Games
for Couples

INTRODUCTION

Purpose

This book is intended to foster the fun, play, and enjoyment that is possible in a sexual relationship between two partners who know each other well. Why is such a book necessary? After all, spontaneity and playfulness seem to be part of the very nature of sexual activity. Sadly, however, the joyfulness and foolishness of our childhood often do not carry into the adult world. We must be serious about our lives and make something of ourselves. And, in the busy confusion of our daily routine, we often take sex too seriously as well. In one of the few places where we ought to be able to put aside our demanding tasks and our preoccupation with achievement and goals to just simply be, we often cannot let go of the seriousness which pervades our lives.

The great paradox of modern civilization is that, with all of our labor-saving devices, we live in an increasingly play-deprived society where the percentage of time we spend in work steadily increases at the expense of play. We have neither time nor permission to play. We cannot give ourselves this permission, nor do those who expect us to behave in predictable roles give it to us.

Our play-deprived society is also a sex play-deprived society. We often turn sex into work and accomplishment. One common way of designating sexual intercourse, "making love," seems to have come out of the

Protestant work ethic's obsession with achievement and productivity. Although it may seem natural to mount a defense in favor of sex as play, very little has ever been written in its behalf. For the most part, the ideas about sexuality that we see promoted encourage us to view sex only within a context of love, commitment, symbolic connection, reverence, and the sacred. Certainly sexuality encompasses all of the above. But, while not disparaging these ways of appreciating sex, there is also a healthy way of looking at sex on the model of two three-year-olds discovering each other in the sandbox.

The perspective which inspires this book is one which invites us to fully appreciate the foolish and frivolous side of sex. How we long to find a way to embrace this side of ourselves is reflected in our admiration of the outrageousness of movie characters who seem to have so much fun doing the outlandish and the ridiculous without a thought as how it might look like to others. What is it that holds us back from fully enjoying ourselves in play and fun with our partners? I think it is simply our lack of imagination, coupled with a certain amount of awkwardness in sexual communication.

Many of us had great fun playing sex games as children until we were caught and made to feel ashamed or punished in other ways. Modern Western societies do not encourage sexual experimentation in the naturally most playful ages of life. By the time we become adults and sexual behavior is expected of us, we may well have lost our sense of play, as well as having forgotten what the best games were and how to initiate them. In that painful transition known as adolescence, we learned a game known as Flirtation, another called Seduction, and a third called Making-Out. As adults though, this repertoire is simply too limiting. We often do not know who we are as sexual beings and what is most enjoyable for us in playful partnership with another person. As we learn more about our sexuality, we look back with painful memories on our earlier sexual relationships and regret that we did not know then what we know now about what pleases us sexually. Many of us started our social lives unnecessarily inhibited in the range of our sexual activities. This becomes clear when we later throw off these inhibitions and wonder how we could have clung to them for as long as we did.

There are very few places where we can go and actually learn about the varieties of sexual behavior and where we fit into this vast spectrum of possibilities.* Sometimes we are fortunate enough to have intimate partnerships with individuals who become our teachers in this sphere. With amazement we discover whole new continents of sexual ecstasy and excitement we never knew were on the map. We are then like ancient mariners who, thinking the earth must be flat, instead find a immense new world on the other side of the ocean. The suspicion grows that every individual is a vast undeveloped resource of sexual possibilities and delights just waiting for permission to be expressed. If only we had guides to instruct us in how to wisely and safely explore our sexuality.

Of course, there are our modern manuals of sexual technique. As helpful as such books may be in giving us permission to try new things with a partner, there is something lacking in their approach. This is how to initiate experimenting with our lovers without coming on like the Marquis de Sade, a Marine Corps drill sergeant, the Wicked Witch of the West, or Maureen O'Hara in a bad mood. These are just our negative fantasies of how our partners will perceive us if, suddenly and out of the blue, we suggest some new practice which they have not tried and may know little about. But these fantasies are enough to inhibit our communication about our longing to explore the new and uncharted realms of our own uncertain desires. By not fully exploring our own desires or those of our partners, we run the risk of having a secure and loving relationship and yet still miss part of the joyous possibility that exists for us, namely, the fit between our own unexplored desires and theirs.

I offer this work as a springboard to a new, frivolous, and foolish way of thinking about sexuality. Do not take this book too seriously. It is all meant to be instructive entertainment. I hope it provides a playful medium for sexual exploration and experimentation in which discovery and sexual delight go hand in hand. The real invitation which this book intends to be just says, "Have fun and let's play." For, when all is said and done, fun and play need no philosophical justification.

---

* One notable exception is the Sex, Love, and Intimacy Workshops of the Human Awareness Institute. See the end of the book for more information on the Human Awareness Institute.

Working Assumptions for a Games Approach to Sexuality

A fun and games approach to sexuality, even from a playful point of view, might raise some red flags in our minds. After all, have we not been taught that playing games with our partners is harmful and destructive of loving communication? We can, however, make an important distinction between healthy and unhealthy, and conscious and unconscious games. The destructive sense of game is a situation where people are acting deceptively with respect to their true intentions and motives. The idea of a game that is being promoted in this book, on the other hand, is more a game on the order of bridge, gin rummy, tennis, or chess. What makes these latter activities healthy is that, for the most part, they are consensual activities where both partners agree without coercion that they are going to play a game of a specific sort. Also, there are well-defined rules to govern whose move it is and to make sure that everyone gets a fair turn. Lastly, there is a definite end to the game when it is agreed that the game is now over and the two people will go back to a less formal and structured way of relating. If you observe these three criteria for healthy games: consensuality of participation, well-defined rules, and a definite beginning and ending point for the game, then playing the games in this book can increase healthy communication and the love in your relationship.

There might still be some anxiety though about playing games whose expressed purpose is discovery and experimentation with sexuality. This anxiety is well expressed in the myth of Pandora. If you will recall, Pandora was given responsibility for a certain box which the gods instructed her never to open under any circumstances. But, being a mere mortal,

Pandora quickly succumbed to curiosity and opened the box. And most of what emerged from the box was unpleasant, to say the least. The fear, then, is that, once we begin this journey of exploration of the outlands of our sexual desires, there is no telling in what perverted country we may end up. What about all those warty trolls, giants, orcs, and demons who lurk in the darkest recesses of our minds? There may be some danger in exploring ourselves, as well as adventure and the glory of discovery.

However, we are on fairly solid ground with respect to undesirable possibilities. For the exploration of our natures, which we are undertaking through the games, is a carefully designed experiment. We are going to see in what ways we might want to expand the margins and boundaries of our sexual possibilities, but we are not out to obliterate these margins and boundaries in a wholesale fashion. The games are designed to give us an opportunity to examine different possibilities to see if they fit with our already existing repertoire of behavior. What does not fit, for whatever reasons of preference, style, or disinterest, can simply be discarded and forgotten. In the process of trying out new possibilities, we become stronger in knowing what it is that we genuinely like and do not like. Some possibilities that we thought we might enjoy exploring more fully may simply fade away after a firsthand look and no longer seem desirable to us. Others, in which we had only an inkling of an interest in before, may come more to the center of our attention and be sources of continual delight and elaboration. In any case, there are probably not many major issues about our sexual desires and interests of which we are totally unaware and which will overwhelm us with surprise. And, should such a major issue emerge, it is much healthier to make an effort to integrate that element into our personality, or to come to terms with it in other ways, so that it is no longer that dark secret on the fringes of our mind, waiting for an opportunity to emerge at an inappropriate time.

This book of games does not claim to be a comprehensive survey of what is sexually possible for a human being. For example, it assumes that the players are a two-person partnership in a comfortable intimacy with each other. There are plenty of other interactive materials, books, and board games designed to explore sexuality with groups of three or more. Some of the games here could be played with more than two players, but the intent of this book is to provide some exploratory tools for couples. Moreover, I have made an effort to focus for the most part on sexual possibilities which are closer to, rather than further away from, the normal range of sexual behavior.

An assumption that I am not making in this book is that every couple is a heterosexual relationship involving one male and one female. There is undoubtedly some male bias in this book and heterosexual bias reflecting my own limited experience. However, with some few exceptions, I have avoided designating roles in the games specifically for the male partner or the female partner.* This is not only to allow for same sex couples but also to explore the wonder and joy of breaking out of stereotypical male and female role expectations in sexual contexts. In most cultures, the man is traditionally expected to be the aggressive initiator and the woman the passive and submissive receiver. With any couple, however, gender does not automatically dictate who will be the more assertive or aggressive sexual partner. In any case, it is great fun to vary the roles so that, even if one partner traditionally takes on the initiator or assertive role in a sexual situation, that partner can take a delightful holiday from the expectation that this is how it always has to be between the two of you.

If you read through this book from start to finish, you will notice that several games are similar in focus and objective. The purpose of this overlap is to allow players an opportunity to access the wonderful resources of their sexuality from slightly different points of view. If one approach does not work for you, perhaps a slightly different version will.

Any of the games that involve role play can be played either as a direct role play, where one or both of the partners actively take on a different persona and act that out in the sex play, or it can be done just as an internal

---

* I hope that creativity and imagination will be sufficient
to overcome any apparent limitations that gender specific
games present to same sex couples in this book.

fantasy. In other words, you don't have to play out the roles directly and overtly for each other; you can experience them as an inward event, or you could even go back and forth between acting out a role play and having it as a fantasy. Be sure to communicate with your partner though about your wish to actively play a role or just to have it as a fantasy so that the expectations will be clear going into a particular game.

If you are finding difficulty making specific times in your busy schedules to play the games, make dates with your partner to play some games from this book. In this way you can set aside a special time to explore each other outside of the normal demands of your work and home schedule.

Rules to Play By

With regard to our most worthy intention to embrace foolishness and cast off the spirit of seriousness, there are still some guidelines and ground rules for rewarding gamepersonship that must be considered. For if we are to abandon ourselves to our inner three-year-old selves, we still need a safe boundary of adult supervision consciousness which will allow us to let go without unnecessary anxiety or fear.

If a particular game is not appealing to you and your partner, skip it and go on to another game. You always have a choice about playing or not playing any of the games. You might find that you want to improvise on some of the instructions or even make up your own game using one in this book as an inspiration. This will also be perfectly O.K. Remember, the focus here is on fun, discovery, joy, play, and spontaneity. Although the rules and guidelines were carefully crafted to facilitate exploration and discovery, you and your partner are the final best judge about what works or does not work for you in a particular game.

Be particularly aware of any potential safety risks to your partner in any game. The games in this book are very low risk in this respect, but before you play a game be aware of potential safety hazards. Also observe sound safe sex practices and good sexual hygiene whenever this becomes relevant in any game.

And, last and not least, always respect what your lover wants to do with regard to playing or not playing any particular game. Never play without your partner's consent. Also, do not play any of the games until you are sure that both of you have a clear understanding of how a particular game is going to be played.

In this regard there are a couple of code words that it is strongly recommended that you adopt before playing any game. The first code word will be called a game termination word. You might use the word "red," for example, to indicate that a particular game is not working for you, and you want to completely end the game and return to your normal way of relating with your partner. Code words are essential when you are engaged in a role play with your partner and you want to stop. The words "stop" or "no" are not good code words, incidentally, because they may well be appropriate in the context of a particular role play. You want to communicate in a decisive and immediate fashion with your partner that this game is not working for you so that it can be ended immediately. Use the game termination word for situations where you want a quick and immediate end to whatever game you are playing.

Sometimes, however, in the course of a game, you may feel like you want to give your partner feedback about some aspect of a game yet still want to continue playing. For this purpose use another code word, a game alteration code word, such as "yellow." This tells your lover that specific changes need to be made to make the game better for you. If you were involved in a role play, for example, and your partner was rough with you in a way that was not arousing, then this would be a time to use the game alteration word so that you can give your partner this particular input and continue with the game. These words are time-outs that you can use to temporarily suspend the play or stop completely, if necessary.

Even if you are in a complete receiver role in a particular game, then, you still have control over what happens with respect to your own comfort and desire to continue the game. No matter what the instructions say about being entirely receptive or letting your partner completely dictate what happens next, remember that the game alteration and game limitation code words always apply and you can bring them into play whenever you want. There is no time in any game when either of the lovers do not have complete control over the game as far as altering the way that it is played or ending it completely is concerned.

Several games request that you blindfold your partner. The purpose for this is to take away our normal reliance on the visual sense for information. With our eyes closed, our sense of touch is more acute as are our senses of hearing and smell. Comfortable blindfolds can usually be obtained in large drug store chains as sleep aids.

In many of the games, a request is made for one partner to be in a totally receiving mode. The purpose of this strategy is to allow one partner to fully focus their attention on sensual and sexual enjoyment and discovery without having to do anything active at all. If it is difficult for you to let yourself go and just receive, remember that you are giving your lover a wonderful opportunity to explore sex and play in a delightful new way. Surrender to the love that you are experiencing and give your partner the truly special gift of really receiving them.

May great joy, happiness, and fulfillment grace your lives together in every minute of every day.

Let the games begin!

FOR PLAY
150 Sex Games
for Couples

Tenderness
Game 1

Select a beautiful romantic piece of music to play. One partner is chosen as the receiver, the other person is then the active partner. Assist each other in playfully removing all of your clothing. Sit on the floor facing each other. Wrap your legs around your partner with the taller person's legs on top and put your arms around the back of your lover. Begin by making eye contact with your beloved. Without doing anything at all, just maintain eye contact for as long as it is enjoyable for you.

Then the person who is to be the active partner first takes their finger tips and lightly strokes the face of their beloved while maintaining eye contact. Touch only the face, the hair, and the neck of your partner.

After touching your partner in this way for a few minutes, the active person then cups their lover's head in their hands and gently and softly kisses them all over their face saying as they do so, "I love you little Susie" or "Joe," etc. After kissing the face of your beloved, whisper in their ear other endearing words of appreciation as you tell your lover how wonderful it is to share sweet moments of intimacy with them, and what it is about them that gives you particular happiness and joy.

Then it is the other partner's turn to receive.

Love Maps
Game 2

The idea of "Love Maps" is to make a map of your lover's erotic body areas. Select one person to receive first. The person who is to receive first lies down in a comfortable position either on their stomach or on their back. Assist your partner in taking off their clothes. Use a blindfold to block out visual cues for the receiver. The active partner then begins to stimulate various parts of their lover's body. Start with light touches and then kiss and lick your partner. Begin anywhere you wish with your stroking and kissing, but be sure to cover the entire body on both sides.

As you touch and kiss your partner, they call out elevations as if you were making a topographical map of your lover's body. The elevations correspond to different degrees of erotic sensitivity. Zero elevations stand for no sensitivity, and valleys, turn off zones, are also noted. Each partner gets a turn receiving in this game.

Heaven
Game 3

There is a story about hell. In hell everyone is given long spoons with which to eat. But no one can get any food because the spoons are so long that the damned cannot get them to their mouths, and so they suffer perpetual frustration and hunger.

In heaven, on the other hand, people feed each other. In this game you make your partner their very favorite meal. Then very lovingly, proceed to feed each other one little bite at a time. No utensils are allowed.

Piggy
Game 4

This little piggy went to the bedroom. In this game you devote loving attention to the feet during sex play. Select one partner to be the receiver. The active person very slowly and sensuously removes all of their lover's clothing and then their own. Have your partner lie down in a comfortable position on their back. From a pan of warm water that you have prepared, bath your lover's feet. Then dry them using your softest towel.

Lift the foot of your beloved and hold it against your body as you stroke it lightly. Then take your lover's foot in your hand and, holding it tenderly up to your face, stroke the foot with your cheek, your forehead, and your hair. Playfully lick the soles of your partner's feet. Try sucking the toes one at a time and several at a time. Put your tongue in between the toes, and if you have a petite partner, put your lover's entire foot in your mouth.

Complete this game by holding both of your lover's feet to your breast as you gently rock the legs back and forth. Play piggy both during foreplay and (creatively) during intercourse.

Great Sex
Game 5

Partners take turns asking each other the question, "What is great sex?" If you are the person answering the question, be sure to say the first thing that comes to your mind without trying to think about what the answer should be. This is a repeated question game, so ask your lover the same question again after the first response, and again after the second response, and so forth, for about two minutes before switching roles. After the game discuss with your partner ways you can integrate what was said into your love play.

Overlaid
Game 6

In this game you both get laid (on). Start by having one partner slowly remove the clothing of the other person. Then reverse roles until no clothes remain. One partner lies down on their back with their lover on top of them. Maintain eye contact with your partner. Lie making eye contact with your beloved for as long as it is enjoyable for you. Then have the person who is on top reverse their body so that the two of you are now lying head to toe. Kiss your lover's feet (see Game #4, "Piggy"). You may have to take turns with this if you are of very different lengths. Do this for as long as you like.

Then the person on the bottom turns over so that they are now lying on their stomach. Their partner then lies on their lover's back with each person facing in the same direction. The person on top gently rocks their body back and forth over their lover's body. Do this for as long as you like, then reverse directions so that the person on top is now lying at their lover's feet. Again, rock your body for your mutual enjoyment.

Then the partner on top turns over so that you are now lying butt to butt. Wiggle around in this position and enjoy the feeling. Then the top partner turns around so that you are back to back facing in opposite directions. Both lovers get a turn being on the bottom.

Breast Friends
Game 7

The person who is the receiver in this game agrees to be in a totally receptive posture for the duration of the game and to make no active movements of their own. Begin by blindfolding the receiving partner. Slowly and tenderly remove all of your lover's clothing and then your own. The receiving partner is assisted in lying down in a comfortable position on their back. The active partner then uses their breasts to caress their lover's body in a loving and sensual way. Pay particular attention to the more sensitive parts of the body as you rub your breasts against your lover's face, into their arm pits, along the sides of the ribs, between their legs, across the genitals, over the arms and hands, and over the feet. Pretend that you do not have any hands and use your breasts as the expressive extensions of your body.

If you are a male and are playing the active role, notice the erotic sensitivity of your own breasts as you stimulate your beloved from head to toe. Each partner gets a turn receiving in this game.

Mirrors
Game 8

Set up some big mirrors in your bedroom so that you can see yourself and your partner making love from different angles. Mirrors on the ceiling are also great if you can arrange it. Then really look at yourselves during your love play. This game can be played in delightful and joyful combination with many of the other games.

Commercials
Game 9

You and your partner set yourselves up somewhere that you can be naked, warm, and comfortable, and also see the television set. Every time there is a commercial, make out for the duration of the commercial, and then stop when the program comes back on again.

The lovers agree to play every one of the games in the *Sex Games for Couples* book. It probably would be a good idea to start somewhere near the beginning of the book and work forward sequentially as some of the later games are a little more challenging than the ones at the beginning. But start anywhere you wish. 21.4 weeks would mean playing one game per day, so space out the games at your own pace. Some of the games require an extended time frame to complete, so be sure to spend as much time on any game as you want to really explore it.

21.4 Weeks
Game 10

Often what we focus our attention on tends to show up more in our experience. Applying this principle to sex play, we are after some fun way to record the wonderful manifestations of our sexual experiences.

One simple way to do this is to get a big jar. Each time you make love with your partner, you put in a penny. Soon you can delight in how much love you have shared with your partner as the pennies accumulate.

Another idea is to record the different new things that you try out with each other. For example, write down the names of the games that you have played together in the *Sex Games for Couples* book or list the sexual variations you have tried in conjunction with this book or from other sources.

Scorekeeper
Game 11

Have You Ever?
Game 12

Say to your partner, "Have you ever . . . ?" Use something outrageous for the blank like, "Have you ever made love in an elevator?" Your lover says, "Oh, yes, I've done that," and they go on to describe in graphic detail that particular sexual trick whether they ever done it or not. Then you guess whether or not they are telling the truth. If you guess correctly, it is a point for you, otherwise it is a point for your partner. Take turns being the questioner.

Cremasteric
Game 13

The cremasteric reflex is a connection between nerves in the inner thigh and muscle tissue of the scrotum. By stroking the inner thigh of your male partner, you can see a reflex movement of the scrotum. This game is best played when your male friend is in a totally receiving mode in a particular game. Do it just for fun to see what happens, or play this game in conjunction with other games where you are gauging your lover's reactions and erotic sensitivities.

Love Strategy
Game 14

In "Love Strategy" you try to determine the most effective way to make your partner feel loved. For some people it is something you do for them that makes them feel loved like making them dinner, buying flowers, remembering anniversaries, and so forth. For other people it is something you say to them such as, "I love you." For many people it is some special way they like to be touched, a specific way of being hugged or kissed, for example.

Begin by remembering a time when you felt especially loved. If you can't recall a specific memory, imagine what it would be like to really be loved in the special way that works best for you. Be very specific in describing how you really like to feel loved after you have narrowed down which of the three modes of communication are most right for you. Then ask your partner to express love for you in just that special way. Each partner gets a turn in this game.

Feel free to play the game again to identify a second or a third favorite love strategy.

Chiropractor
Game 15

One person is selected to be the receiver and lies on their stomach in a comfortable position after they have been tenderly undressed by their lover. Their partner then begins to make love to them focusing all of their attention on their partner's back from neck to bum.

Begin by lightly stroking your lover's back. Tap your fingers lightly all over your partner's back as if you were playing the piano or typing. Kiss and lick your lover's back from end to end and from side to side. By sighing, groaning, or moaning, the receiver partner indicates which parts of their back are the most sensitive. Stroke your lover's back with your beard and/or hair. If you lack hair on your head, stroke your partner's back with the skin of your conveniently bare head. Use your forearms to make broad strokes over their back. Lie in a crosswise position over your partner and lightly stroke your beloved's back with your torso and breasts.

After stroking your partner's body in this way, you might wish to use massage oil on the back of your beloved. By using oil you can apply more pressure with less friction.

Thighs and Whispers Game 16

Your attention is going to be focused on your partner's thighs from crotch to knee in this game. Select which partner is going to be the receiver, then slowly and sensually undress your lover. Have them lie down in a comfortable position while you blindfold them. Avoid all direct genital contact for the entire duration of the game. Where the legs join the torso is a fair target, however, and you begin your stroking from this wonderful crease of love down to the kneecaps.

Begin by just very gently stroking your partner's thighs from crease to knee using very light strokes. Spend some minutes just lightly stroking your lover in this way making sure all parts of their thighs are touched again and again. Your partner's moans and sighs indicate that this is very sensual and erotic for them, but you avoid the temptation to touch or kiss their genitals.

It is very important for the receiving partner to remain totally receptive throughout this game and not make any active movements to accelerate the love play in a genital direction. When you reach the knees, be sure to stroke underneath the kneecaps.

Next, using the hair on your head, stroke your lover's thighs with your hair and with your beard, if you have one. Should you perhaps not have any hair on your head, use the conveniently bare skin of your crown to stroke your partner. If the active partner is a male, use the hair on your chest to stroke the thigh.

A woman partner can stroke the thigh with her breasts. Use the broad surfaces of your forearms to stroke your lover's thighs. Next, nuzzle your lovers thighs with your face from kneecap to crease, and back again.

Finally, kiss and lick your partner starting with the underside of their knees and playfully working your way up to their crease. When you reach the crease, spend a lot of time licking this area. Proceed on to other games only when you have completely loved every inch of each thigh.

**Earsies
Game 17**

In this game the ears are the focus of sensual and erotic attention. One partner is selected to receive and agrees to keep their eyes closed throughout the course of the game. (A blindfold may get in your way here.) The active partner then kisses and strokes their lover's ears attempting to wake up the slumbering sensual giant in this part of the body. Ear lobes like to be pulled, kissed, licked, and sucked. The various folds of the ear can be lightly massaged and stretched to good effect. Place you hands lightly over your partner's ears as you kiss their face. A wet tongue in the ear may be too intense for your lover, so experiment with putting other body parts (nipples, for example) into the ear.

**Tom Jones
Game 18**

This game was inspired from a scene in the movie *Tom Jones* in which there is a voluptuous eating scene. A beautiful dinner is prepared by either one or both of the lovers. A dinner setting is prepared on a special low table at which the partners sit on cushions. There is candlelight and delightfully soft music in the background. Once the meal is prepared, the lovers take off all of their clothes and enjoy the meal in naked and lusty anticipation of enjoying each other afterwards.

Sleeping Beauty
Game 19

For "Sleeping Beauty" you must get your partner's agreement to participate in advance of the actual event. Play "Sleeping Beauty" when you are in bed sleeping with your lover. The active player is the one who happens to be awake at whatever hour that happens to be. The receiving partner is the one who is sound asleep.

The active person awakens the sleeper by beginning foreplay and sexual arousal. Begin very slowly and gently to stimulate your lover with very light touch and see how far you can get before they fully awaken. Once they are awake, go on to other games.

Chin Rest
Game 20

The objective of "Chin Rest" is to awaken the erotic sensitivity of the perineum (the area between the genitals and the anus). Like an undiscovered sex goddess or sex god, the perineum lies in that forgotten realm betwixt and between. The erotic potential of this region sometimes needs some directed sensual attention before it fully awakens.

Select one partner to be the receiver and playfully take off their clothes. Have your lover lie on their back and roll their legs up to a ninety degree angle. The receiver holds their legs so that the position is not uncomfortable to maintain. Then the active partner gently strokes the perineum with their fingertip as they receive feedback from their lover about how it feels. Tongue tips are also used to titillate this area as well as knotted strings, fabrics of different kinds, soft pieces of wood, feathers, brushes, cold pieces of metal, and sometimes even ice cubes. The pressure of the chin on this area can also be very stimulating.

**Car Wash
Game 21**

This is a game for the shower. One of the lovers puts lavish amounts of soap all over their body. Then standing together in the shower, the lathered person proceeds to "wash" the unlathered partner by rubbing bodies together. Be sure to include washing back to back and front to back, as well as front to front.

**Fingernails
Game 22**

For "Fingernails" you will need two sets of press-on nails. Begin by slowly and sensuously taking off your partner's clothing until none remains for each of you. Enjoy putting the fingernails on your partner. If you wish paint your lover's new nails. Gently blindfold the partner who is to be the first receiver.

The active partner then begins a slow tactical exploration of their lover's body, touching with only the nails. Begin at the feet and slowly work your way up to the head of your partner. Auditory responses to the sensations may be given but no words may be used. After the whole body is explored, the roles are reversed.

**Body Parts
Game 23**

Write the names of various body parts on slips of paper and put them into a hat or a bowl. Each player draws out one slip. He or she proceeds to make love to that part of the body for at least ten to fifteen minutes and gives loving attention only to that portion of their body. The other partner then draws a slip and does the same.

I've Got A Secret
Game 24

One partner starts the game by saying, "I've got a secret." The player's partner then has twenty questions to discover what their lover's secret is. The secret is always about some special type of sexual favor that they would like. Ask as specific or as general a question as you like of your partner, but the questions have to be framed in such a way that the only possible answers are "yes" or "no." Each partner gets a turn being the one questioned in this game.

Love Braille
Game 25

Both you and your partner begin by securely blindfolding yourselves so that neither of you can see anything. Start with all of your clothes on. Then one partner slowly begins to undress their lover. Take turns taking off one piece of clothing at a time from each other. During this game no spoken words are allowed but communicate freely with your partner through moans, sighs, groans, and hurrahs. Proceed to make wild, glorious love as you fully experience and celebrate your lover through the nonvisual senses.

Kissey Face
Game 26

Sit in a comfortable position with your partner so that you can easily make eye contact. The leg straddle position is very convenient for this with each person's legs wrapped around their lover's waist, and with the tallest person's legs on top. Begin by letting yourself dive into your partner's eyes. Be fully present with their gaze until you can see the spiritual essence of who they really are. When you have looked as long as you wish into your partner's eyes, let your own eyes close. If your partner closes their eyes first, then let your own close as well. Keep your eyes closed for the remainder of the game.

Choose one partner to go first. That person then begins to kiss their lover's face all over. Be sure to kiss the eyelids lightly, and below the lower lip, and between the nose and the lip. Kiss your partner as long as you wish, then switch so that your lover is now kissing you in the same way. After receiving the kisses for a blissful eternity, the partner who began the kissing lightly grazes lips with their beloved. Keeping your mouths closed, very gently kiss each other's lips. The person who began kissing then takes their tongue and parts their partner's lips with it. Their lover responds by touching their tongue to their partner's tongue. After tongues explore each other, let your tongues explore the insides of each other's mouths. Use your teeth to gently stimulate your lover's mouth areas. Then abandon yourselves to wild, passionate kissing for at least thirty minutes before you do anything else overtly sexual.

♥ ♥ ♥

Scratcher
Game 27

No, this is not a lotto game, even though a good partner is worth more than a wagon full of gold. Assist each other in taking off your clothes. Then lie with your lover, with the person selected to be the receiver on top. The active partner then proceeds to lightly scratch the back of their lover, receiving verbal feedback at every point about how much pressure is desired. After backs are scratched, go on to other parts of the body and see what pleasurable sensations can be generated in this way. Then reverse roles so that the active person is now the receiver.

Armies
Game 28

In preparation for this game, deodorants were scrupulously avoided by each partner. Also, any rings or other jewelry on the hand or wrist have been removed.

Select one person to be the receiver and have your lover lie down in a comfortable position while they are blindfolded. The active person then begins to seduce their partner with love play which focuses on the arms and hands.

Take your partner's arm and pull it conveniently away from their body to expose their armpit. Nuzzle your lover's armpit with your nose and tickle the hair under their arm as you drink in the wonderful sex scent of your lover. Begin to kiss and lick the upper arm paying particular attention to the inside of the arm. By moans, groans, and sighs the receiving partner lets you know which are the most sensitive and sensual areas for them.

Continue to kiss and lick your way down the arm until you reach the hand. At this point pick up your lover's hand and hold it to your face so that you can lovingly stroke their hand with your face. Kiss and lick the palm of the hand. Lick between each finger and then slowly and deeply suck each finger one at a time into your mouth. Put your partner's hand on your breast and stroke their arm from armpit to fingers with slow, gentle, sensual strokes. Then proceed to the other arm and enjoy it in the same way.

Play this game over a period of at least ten sessions of love play with your partner. During each session one of you is in charge of interrupting your normal love-making pattern. The person in charge of doing this alternates with each session. Be sure to change at least one thing that you normally do with each other each time you enjoy sex together. It might be making love in a new place in your home, or in a new position, or varying the order in which you normally do things in foreplay. It could be stroking your partner in a new way or in a place on their body that is usually not given much attention. The partner who is the initiator of the variation directs their lover through whatever new thing you are going to do.

**Variation
Game 29**

In "Gossip" you take turns describing the sexy escapades of someone else. This can be either a real or an imaginary person. If a real person is used as protagonist, be sure your partner knows that you are playing Game #30 of the *Sex Games for Couples* book and not talking about a real event. Try to make your description as sexy and exciting as possible. Start off by saying something like, "Do you know what I heard about Mary Sue?" "No, please tell me." "Well, I heard that last week she was with three guys and she . . . ."

**Gossip
Game 30**

Waterfall
Game 31

You and your partner make love under a waterfall in this game. Since waterfalls are often not conveniently located close to where you live, use the shower instead. You might begin by washing each other in the shower. (See Game #21, "Car Wash.") Gradually you find that the soap begins to dwell on erotic areas of the body. (Avoid getting soap into the vagina.) Before long, cleanliness is the last thing on your mind.

If the water is not a sufficient lubricant, use a petroleum based lubricant. Petroleum based lubricants cannot be used with condoms.

Nuzzler
Game 32

Select one of you to be the active partner in this game. This person then pretends that some misfortune has rendered them unable to use either their hands or their feet. Fortunately, however, this person has their nose, face, and head as parts of their body that they can freely control and use for love play. The "nuzzler" proceeds to make love to their partner using only these parts and their tongue. Begin this game with lots of delicious foreplay. Cover the entire body of your lover with creative nuzzling before proceeding to the genitals.

Rain Game
Game 33

Wait until a good rain comes to wherever you happen to be. Lie down together where you can hear the rain coming down and slowly and sensuously make love to your partner while listening to the sound of the rain. If it happens to be a warm summer night, you might want to chance making love in the rain outside.

For nine and one-half weeks, you and your partner explore different games in the *Sex Games for Couples* book. At the conclusion of the nine and one-half weeks, you plot a ten minute peak experience with your lover. Pick some time when you are under some kind of deadline. You only have a little bit of time to get to the meeting or appointment. You come home for lunch and you have to go back in ten minutes. The pizza delivery man is expected. See what joyful wonderment you can create with your lover in just ten minutes of sex fun.

9 and 1/2 Weeks Plus Ten Minutes Game 34

You and your partner take turns playing Santa Claus. Only in this case you are very naughty little boys and girls. Instead of a list of gifts and toys that you want for Christmas, you make up a list of sexual variations and sexual fantasies that you want to try out.

Each person makes their list separately from their partner. Do not be concerned about how much or how little is on your sheet. As long as you have something on your list, you can play Christmas over and over again. Share your list with your lover and work in partnership with them to create what it is that you want. Start with any items that are the same on each list. Then take turns doing one thing from each person's sheet.

After you finish your first list, start the game over again with an additional list which has grown more precise and detailed from the explorations that you did together with the initial sheet.

Christmas Game 35

One of you is selected as the receiver and is blindfolded. The active partner begins by lightly kissing and stroking their lover's face, head, and hair. Then the person who is playing the active role begins to kiss and lick their lover's neck. Every square inch of your partner's neck is covered with kisses and licks. Begin with soft gentle kisses, then make another tour of your lover's neck with more forceful wet kisses, and then a third round with even more forceful and aggressive kisses. Conclude the game with very gentle bites, but be careful not to leave bruises.

Reformed Vampires Game 36

For "Slippy Sliddy Widdey" you need an open floor space, some kind of a mat to put on the floor (an exercise mat, for example), and several old sheets to put on the mat. You might want to put a shower curtain or something similar between your sheets and the mat.

Assist your partner in taking off all of your clothes. One person is selected as the first receiver and lies down on the sheets while their lover pours oil all over their body, rubbing them playfully all over as they do so. You can use scented massage oil for this purpose. Once the first partner is totally oiled, switch roles and have the oiled person apply oil to their lover in the same fashion. When you are both totally lubricated, have outrageous fun rolling on top of each other. This game is a good lead-in to Game #6, "Overlaid."

Slippy Sliddy Widdey Game 37

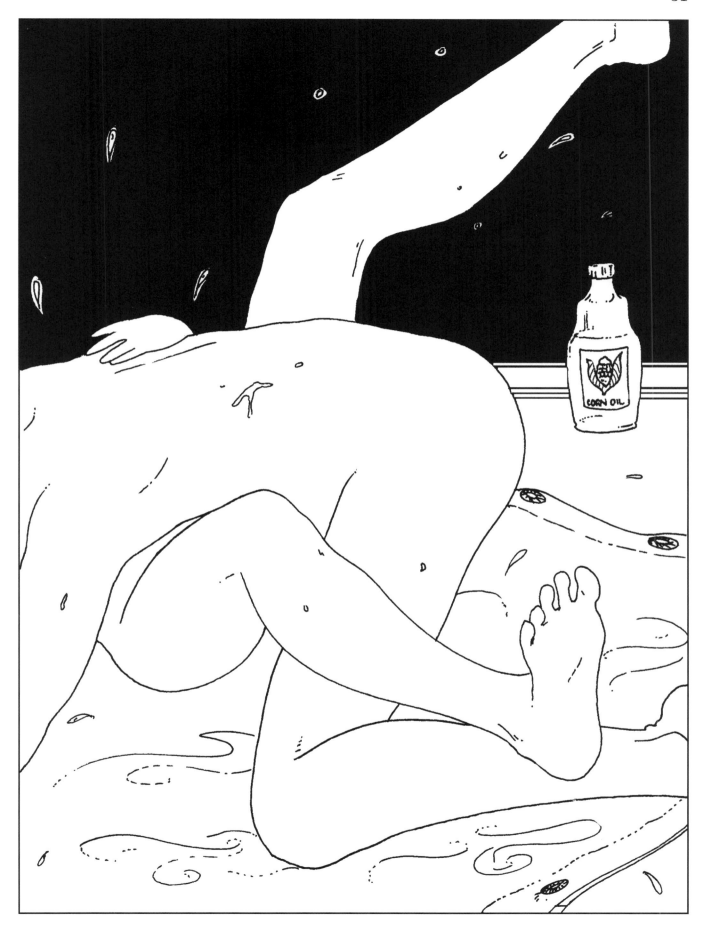

This time even though Little Red Riding Hood does get eaten up, she gets treated with respect by the Big Bad Wolf. Playfully assist each other in removing all of your clothes. One person is selected to go first and lies in a comfortable position on their back. Their partner then experiences a sudden and complete case of amnesia with respect to how to pleasure their lover orally. Fortunately the reclining partner is very explicit and specific in communicating just exactly what they want their lover to do at every point as they give continuous feedback. The active partner does only what they are instructed to do. Then the roles are reversed.

Little Red Riding Hood
Game 38

Select a really good vintage wine or some other beverage that you and your partner both enjoy. The active person takes a mouthful of the wine or other drink and then kisses their lover without swallowing. Slowly the wine is squirted into their partner's mouth. Then the roles are switched, and the active person becomes the receiver so that they can receive some wine from their lover's mouth.

Wine Taster
Game 39

For "Nibbler" you need lots of little pieces of fruit or chocolate. Honey, chocolate syrup, or whipped cream can also be used. Place the goodies in or on strategic parts of your partner's body and then proceed to nibble them off. Good spots include armpits, navels, stomachs, thighs, backs, splits between buns, creases between legs and genitals, penises, outer lips, inner lips, nipples, between toes, hanging between the lips of the mouth, and so forth.

Nibbler
Game 40

At some regular interval of time (like every Friday, for example), you and your partner agree to tell each other at least one dirty joke. (You can cheat and tell nondirty jokes if you want.) Buy a joke book and read through it to be prepared when your time comes.

Dirty Joke
Game 41

Begin "Sex Dreams" by playing #19, "Sleeping Beauty." In this case, however, the sleeper refuses to awaken but pretends that they are still asleep throughout the entirety of the tantalizing arousal and ecstatic consummation phase of the love play. When your mutual sexual excitement has reached its peak, whatever that may look like, gently tuck your partner back into the sleeping position they happened to be in before they were so sweetly disturbed.

Sex Dreams
Game 42

One partner is selected to be blindfolded. The other partner then takes one part of their body and rubs it against any portion of their lover's body except their hands. The blindfolded person then tries to guess which part of the body is being used.

Pin the Tit
on the Donkey
Game 43

Hot Tub
Game 44

You and your lover have sexual intercourse in a hot tub in this game. Be sure the children are not going to come home unexpectedly and that you have not forgotten you have invited the neighbors over. Use the buoyancy of the water to support yourselves in the hot tub. One exciting position is for the man to be standing with the woman wrapped around his waist. Experiment with one partner sitting on a ledge with their lover on top.

If water is not sufficient lubrication for your love play, use a petroleum based lubricant. Petroleum based lubricants cannot be used with condoms.

Yellow Pages
Game 45

In "Yellow Pages" you are going to let your fingers do the walking. Select one partner to be the receiver. Slowly and delightfully take off your lover's clothes, have them lie down in a comfortable reclining position, and blindfold them. Touch your partner lightly all over their body and kiss them gently from head to toe.

Then, if your partner is a woman, beginning with only the index finger of one hand, very lightly touch and stroke your partner's genitals with just that one finger. Enjoy the slippery wetness of your excited lover as your finger traces a line down the length of her love organs.

Touch only the outer parts of your partner's love folds at first, and then let the finger slowly slip into the vagina. The receiving person is to assist your explorations with appropriate groans, sighs, and moans indicating what feels the most sensual and exciting to them about what you are doing. Try putting more than one finger into the vagina. Rotate your hand around so that you can touch the vaginal wall in different spots. Be sure your receiving partner is giving you continual feedback about what feels best for them.

After exploring the vagina, slowly withdraw your finger and move in the direction of the clitoris. With just one finger, stroke on either side of the clitoris. Using just the ball of your finger, make very light tapping strokes. Experiment with other very light touches paying particular attention to the sides of your partner's love button.

If the receiving partner is a male, begin in the same way by undressing your lover, putting him in a comfortable reclining position, and blindfolding him. After lightly stroking and kissing your partner from head to toe, let your hands come into proximity with your lover's penis. Begin by lightly squeezing the penis. Without trying to masturbate your partner, lightly stroke his penis and run your fingers along the shaft. Grasp the penis at the base and pull up on the shaft toward the head. Lightly tap the penis as if you were playing a musical instrument or typing.

Grasp the penis in your closed hand and turn it very slowly as you move up from the base of the penis toward the head. Put one finger on the top side of the penis and your thumb on the underside of the head of the penis and jiggle the penis in your hand. Try some very gentle masturbation strokes but not enough to make your lover come. Gently pull the testicles down while you pull the penis up. Lovingly stroke your partner's scrotum and the underside of his testicles.

Remember that genital sensitivity is very different for individual people and may vary considerably for the same person on any given day. Be sure your receiving partner gives you continuous feedback about how the various strokes feel for them on this extremely vulnerable part of the body.

Rocking Chair
Game 46

Most rocking chairs have arms which can get in the way, so an actual rocking chair may not be the best for this game. Find a comfortable chair and have the male partner sit in it. Bring your lover to the fullest possible arousal, then sit on him in the chair. Rock your bodies for mutual ecstasy.

Soccer
Game 47

In "Soccer" you are going to make love to your partner without using your hands or arms. Pretend for the duration of this game that you do not have any hands or arms. However, you do have skillful use of your tongue, legs, toes, head, and torso.

Anticipation
Game 48

In "Anticipation" you are going to intensify your meeting with your lover by something you do apart from each other first. Pick a time when you are separated and use this occasion to sensually and erotically stimulate yourself through masturbation. Bring yourself to a very high peak of arousal, but do not have an orgasm. Then join your lover for some intense sex play.

Puritan Game 49

This game is called "Puritan" because, for at least the beginning of this game, you pretend that the genitals are forbidden areas which cannot be touched with hands or lips. All other parts of the body, however, are fair game for stroking, kissing, licking, and whatever else you can think of. The object of this game is to fully arouse your partner and have intercourse. However, you are not to touch, fondle, lick, or suck your lover's genitals. Be creative and find other ways to bring your partner to full arousal. It is O.K. for other body parts to touch your lover's genitals but not hands or mouths.

Treasure Game 50

In "Treasure" the female partner is the receiver. Have your partner lie down on her back in a comfortable position after you have slowly and sensuously removed all of her clothing. Then blindfold your lover. Kiss your partner lightly and tenderly, and then gently stroke her body from head to toe.

Assist her in raising her legs as you settle in between them. Lightly kiss and stroke the wonderful temple of Venus. Take your index finger and let it play around the clitoris and love folds of your partner for a while. Then let it slide into the opening.

The treasure that we are seeking is called the G-spot. This is a spot of heightened sexual sensitivity located on the upper vaginal wall about one-half to a full index finger's length into the opening. The G-spot usually has a different texture than the surrounding tissue. Begin to stroke the spot gently with your finger by pulling it toward you as if you were beckoning someone to come to you. Ask your lover for feedback about where to press and how hard. Your partner may get a feeling like she needs to urinate when the spot is touched but there is no need for alarm.

In addition to stimulating the G-spot from inside, you can also stroke it from a spot near the top of the pubic bone. Use either your finger or your tongue to massage the G-spot on the outside. Elicit your partner's help in finding

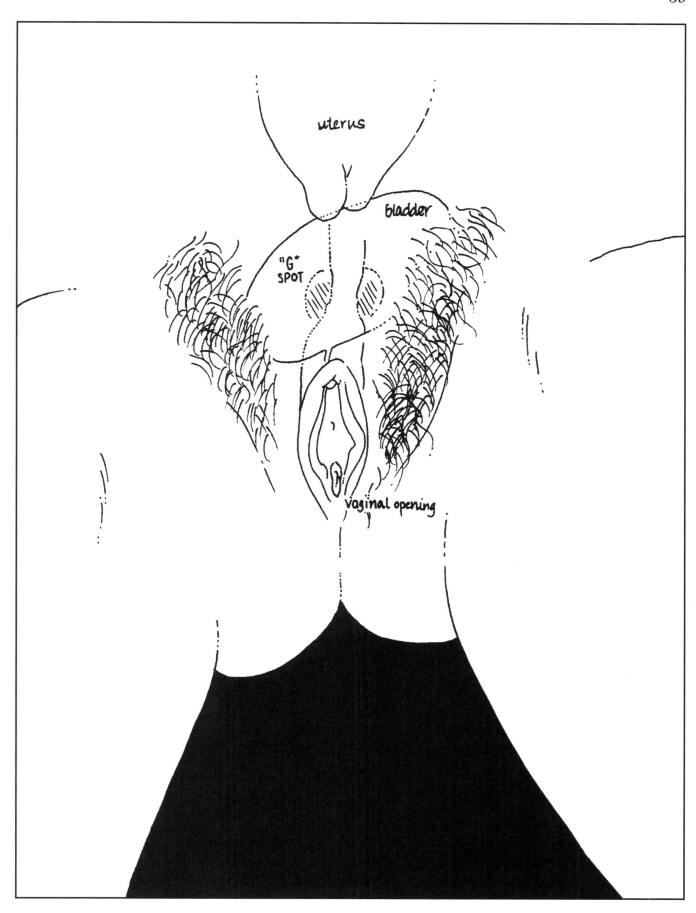

this external stimulation spot. Press in and down with gentle pressure until your partner exclaims "O, Gee!" Play with stroking the spot inside and outside at the same time. Sensitivity of the G-spot can vary a great deal depending on the arousal level of your partner. After you locate the spot, go on to other games.

Be sure that nails are trimmed before playing this game.

True Confessions
Game 51

You and your partner take turns telling each other one of your most compelling and persistent sexual fantasies. Then invent a way to fulfill the fantasy, either by acting the fantasy out directly, or by having your lover role play a scenario that expresses it. In this way you can represent situations that either you do not wish to create or that cannot be constructed. For example, a man has a fantasy of having a magic sex gun that looks like an ordinary ballpoint pen. Whatever unwitting female he clicks it at falls totally under the control of his will. She remembers nothing about the incident later.

Clothies
Game 52

You and your lover make love with some of your clothes on rather than being completely nude. For example, the male partner might pull up the sexy skirt of his lover who is kneeling facing away from him. He then pulls her panties down and has intercourse. Or the woman sits on the man who is naked from the waist down but still wearing his shirt and hat. This game goes really well with any role plays that you might want to enjoy with your partner, as you can dress up in role and then make love with some of your clothing on to reinforce the scene that you want to play.

File Clerks
Game 53

Pretend that you are both filing clerks in some huge office. Through some glorious stroke of luck, you have both been assigned to the basement filing room. This room is very isolated and there is no one else around.

In one version the female part of the pair just happens to bend over a little too provocatively, and her male companion is so overcome by desire that he raises her skirt up and pulls her panties down without any preamble. He then proceeds to full-scale sex play, starting with light touch and oral stimulation of his partner. She does not resist as she is overcome with passion and desire.

In another version the female clerk notices the bulge in her male companion's pants. She stares at his crotch for such a long time that he is virtually transfixed and paralyzed with lust. Sensing that her victim's will is immobilized, she quickly crosses the gap between them and slowly unzips his pants. When his penis springs into her hands, she holds it sensuously for a while before putting it into her mouth . . . .

Pillow Talk
Game 54

The lovers pretend to be teenage girls talking about the boys they have gone out with. There has been some really passionate sex play which they are eager to describe to each other, but they are afraid of getting too detailed at first for fear that their friend will think badly of them. Slowly the truth comes out in full blushing detail as the friends pry the facts out of each other in tantalizing bits and pieces.

Sex, Lies, and Video Tape Game
Game 55

One partner is selected to be the active person. A video camera is set it up so that it is totally focused on the other partner. The initiator then asks their lover very detailed and personal questions about their sexual history. For example, they may ask them: "What is the strangest place you have every made love?" "Describe what it was like to have intercourse for the first time?" or "What really surprising thing have you done sexually that people would never suspect?" The questioner then records everything on videotape.

If you do not have a videotape camera, play the game using a cassette recorder. Each partner gets a turn being the questioner in this game.

Role Reversal
Game 56

The more aggressive and assertive partner in the couple plays the role of Mary Sue. The less aggressive and assertive partner is now Joe. Joe knocks on the door of Mary Sue's hotel room asking to come in to chat. Joe actually has a secret agenda to seduce the very virginal Mary Sue. Foolishly Mary Sue lets Joe in. Joe then proceeds to seduce Mary Sue using his best reluctant virgin techniques. Slowly but surely, Mary Sue succumbs to Joe's irresistible charm.

Photographer
Game 57

One person plays the role of a struggling photographer. The photographer's partner agrees to help him or her shoot a series of erotic images which will be used to promote the career of the fledgling picture maker. Explore and experiment in order to get the most erotic poses possible. Use costumes and props as appropriate to construct the most beautiful sexual images you can envision.

One partner plays the role of the horny doctor, while the other person is the patient. The doctor begins by saying, "Take off your clothes." The doctor then proceeds with a thorough visual examination of the patient having them move their body into revealing positions to help the examination along. The patient directs the doctor to whatever hurts, and the doctor applies soothing and healing touch to that area. Imperceptibly at first, and then undeniably and irresistibly, the touching and soothing becomes more and more erotic until doctor and patient are swept away in a flood tide of passion.

The Incredible Lightness of Being Game
Game 58

Select a very hot X-rated videotape. Begin watching it from different corners of the room. Then after about fifteen minutes, move into a reclining position together, but still keep your clothes on. After another fifteen minutes have elapsed, slowly help each other in taking off your clothes, but do not do anything else. Only when another fifteen minutes have elapsed do you start touching and stroking each other.

Videos
Game 59

Most wilderness focus movies have one delicious scene where the male hero and his woman friend strip naked, swim in the lake, and then, usually out of sight of the camera, presumably make love in the water. This is what you and your lover do in this game. Swimming pools, if they are sufficiently screened from public view, can make great lakes if an actual lake is not available.

If the water is not a sufficient lubricant, use a petroleum based lubricant. Petroleum based lubricants cannot be used with condoms.

Tarzan and Jane
Game 60

Locker Room
Game 61

The partners are both teenage males who talk to each other about their sexual adventures with the local women.

Picnic
Game 62

Pack a delicious picnic lunch and head out for a beautiful and secluded nature spot. You spread your blanket under the glorious sunlight and enjoy your lunch. Later you snuggle on the blanket and look up at the sky. The female partner wears a skirt or dress which makes it easy to enjoy sex without getting completely undressed. The male lover also wears easily accessible clothing. A loaf of bread, a jug of wine, and you.

Virgins
Game 63

You and your partner are virgins. Moreover, you both know for sure that you will end up in hell, forever, if you allow yourselves to go all the way. For the duration of this game, make out passionately but avoid intercourse.

Home Video
Game 64

A video camera is needed for this game. Set up the camera so it can take in your bedroom, and then make your own video record of your joyful celebrations of love together for later enjoyment. You can use the video as the tape you use for Game #59, "Videos," or play it when you are making love so that there are recorded images of your sex play in addition to the real thing.

One person is a well-known sex therapist. The other partner is a client with a special problem. Perhaps the clitoris cannot be located, or maybe the penis has suddenly lost some of its usual sensitivity. You might be so fortunate as to have Dr. Grafenberg as your physician helping you to find his famous spot. You are a very good patient. Be sure to fully and carefully describe the particular problem that you want the good doctor to help you with. The doctor then very patiently assists the patient with ways to enhance their sexual life through a hands-on demonstration.

Sex Therapist
Game 65

One person selects to be the geisha and the other partner is the client. The geisha undresses the client and takes them into the shower or bath where she/he proceeds to lovingly bathe them. Then the geisha gives the client a wonderful massage using scented oils. Later the geisha plays the active role in love-making, while the client just receives it all without having to do anything.

Geisha
Game 66

In "Lusty" you and your lover take turns describing your sexual feelings and desires for each other. With as much intimate and graphic detail as possible, describe what you would like to do with your lover and what it would be like to fully experience special, wonderful, and delicious forms of sex play with them. Tell how much you would delight in undressing your lover or undressing for them, describe the parts of your lover's body that you are most turned on by, how you would shower your lust and affection on those special parts, how you want to tease your lover, play your special love games with them, take them to your special love-making spots, etc. This is a good game to play on the telephone, if you are separated, or through correspondence.

Lusty
Game 67

Lady's Choice
Game 68

The female partner looks through the description of all 150 games and picks out one particular game that she would really love to play. Then the male partner plays this game with her. (If you have another gender configuration, decide who will make the choice.)

Filling in the
Doughnut
Game 69

This is a massage game. One partner is selected to be the receiver and remains in the receptive role throughout the game, making no active motions of their own. The active partner uses a scented oil and begins by pouring small amounts of the oil on their lover's body. Then they proceed to give their partner a wonderful full body massage excluding the genitals. Only after massaging the entire body does the active partner slowly approach the genitals.

Begin by pouring oil on the genitals. See what wonderful sounds of delight you can create in your beloved as you tenderly and sensuously massage their love organs.

Here are hints for massaging the goddess. Begin by placing one hand on your partner's love triangle and the other hand on her heart. Make eye contact with your lover and leave your hands in place for a delicious moment while you establish a heart connection with your beloved. Then rotate your hand over the genitals slowly and gently. See if you can create a connecting stroke where you start with the breasts, and work down to the genitals, and then back again. Facing away from your partner, pull up with your hands across her genitals. Using one or two fingers, very tenderly trace the crease between the outer and the inner lips. Pull gently on the pubic hair. Starting at your lover's thigh, move your hands over the genital area and then back down the leg. Putting your hands in a prayer position and facing away from your partner, stroke the outer lips between your hands as you pull up.

These are hints for massaging Priapus. Use lots of oil on the penis and you can use firmer strokes which he often enjoys. Begin by pulling gently on your lover's pubic hair. Then take your partner's penis in one hand and place the other hand over his heart as you establish eye contact and a heart connection with your lover before you begin. Take the penis in your hands and roll it back and forth like rolling dough. Starting at the base of the penis with one hand on top of the other, pull upward, turning your hands as you do so. Start in the same position with one hand on top of the other, and pull up rapidly from the base of the penis. Holding the penis in one hand just below the head, pull down with first one hand and then the other from this point. Putting one hand over the testicles and one hand encircling the penis, pull up on the penis as you pull down gently on the whole scrotum area. While stroking the penis with one hand, have the other hand make a big circle around the entire area where the genitals connect with the leg. Hold the penis down so it is on its back and take the other hand and stroke down the underside of your lover's penis.

Sensitivity of the genitals varies a great deal from individual to individual and can be different for any one person from day to day. Be particularly sensitive to your partner's input and feedback whenever you are stroking what is the most vulnerable part of the body for most people.

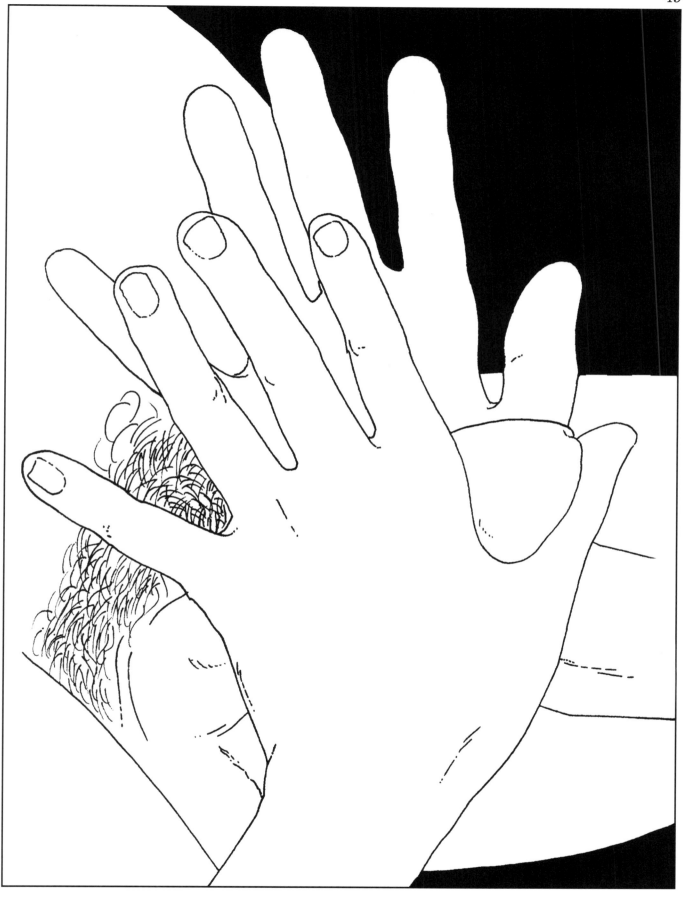

Go to a drive-in movie with your sweetie. Wear lose comfortable clothing suitable for the occasion (no body suits or tight jeans, for example). Pretend that you and your beloved have never been sexually intimate before and this is your big chance to get the ball(s) rolling. As the movie begins, one partner slowly moves close to their lover and puts their arm around them. As the movie progresses, have the active partner take more and more liberties, slowly building the sexual excitement.

Passion Pit
Game 70

The partners spend some joyful time making chocolate truffles, brownies, or something else that ends up with a big bowl full of chocolaty stuff. After you have put your confection in the oven, playfully assist each other in removing all of your clothes. One partner then takes the bowl, which you have conveniently left partly full, and with their finger paints a line of chocolaty goo on their lover's nude body. Then their partner does the same to them. After you are both totally covered in chocolate and the bowl is completely empty, proceed to eat each other off.

Truffles
Game 71

You and your partner pretend that you are playing roles different from your normal everyday selves during love play. In one game, for example, one partner might play the role of the principal with their lover being a student caught in some mischievous activity which merits discipline. Brainstorm with your lover about which roles are going to be the most fun for you. Be sure each person gets a turn creating a script for your role plays.

Role Play
Game 72

Gentleman's Voice
Game 73

The male partner looks through the description of the 150 games and picks out one game that he would really like to play. Then the female partner plays it with him. (If you have another gender configuration, decide who will make the choice.)

Erotic Book
Report
Game 74

At agreed upon time intervals, one partner agrees to report to their lover about one erotic video, erotic short story, or erotic book which they have separately reviewed. They then present part or all of the video for their partner to see. If it is an erotic short story, they read the story to their lover or parts of the erotic book. Then it is the other person's turn to be the reviewer for the next session.

Fantasy Voice
Game 75

In "Fantasy Voice" you make love with your partner while they describe your participation in your favorite fantasy. Choose one partner to be the narrator for their lover's fantasy. One of you begins by telling your lover your favorite fantasy in its entirety. As the love play begins, the partner of the lover who described their fantasy begins to narrate the fantasy as if it were taking place in the immediate moment. "The three bikini-clad goddesses notice you and are driven mad with lust. Without even saying so much as hello, they go right over to where you are lying down, rip off the tops of their bikinis, and begin to rub their bare breasts all over you."

The partner may be just narrating what is happening to their lover or may be an active player in the fantasy itself. The description need not match the actual love play. The narrator may be describing one type of sexual activity while engaging in another. The fantasy can be ahead or behind what is actually happening, but the end of the fantasy is planned to eventually coincide with the completion of the love play in whatever form that takes.

You Name It
Game 76

Imagine that you live in a peculiar country where it is strictly forbidden to learn anything about the physiology and anatomy of a human being. In this strange land, adults grow up without really knowing anything at all about the names of the sexual parts of the other gender. Fortunately you have managed to form a warm friendship with a person of that gender.

In this game you take turns asking each other about your bodies, how they work, and what the different parts are called. Also ask how it feels to be touched and stroked in each delicious little part. Since neither one of you has ever had any sexual education, you invent your own private, personal names for each body part and for each sexual activity. Delight in quizzing each other to find out what each thing is named, what it does, and how it feels using your own private language.

Phone Home
Game 77

Find an answering machine for which no one else but your partner takes the messages. Then, when they least expect it, leave a sexy message on their machine. Describe in graphic detail what you would like to do with them in love play, or what you are going to do with them the next time that you are together. Or have sex with yourself and leave the sounds of this on the machine.

Countdown
Game 78

Determine with your partner a preset amount of time during which you agree not to have intercourse or oral sex. Set the time for some amount which is more than the time that you usually enjoy in foreplay before intercourse. Be sure to keep your agreement not to have intercourse or oral sex before the time period has elapsed.

A good way to keep track of time without relying on clocks and alarms is to play a favorite combination of selections of love-making music. When you have a free moment, time the playing of these pieces of music so that you know how long they take. Then base your time estimate on when the music changes.

Genital Chicken
Game 79

Both partners take off their clothes and proceed to arouse each other in the most provocative ways they can imagine, but always stop short of actual intercourse. The first person to say, "Let's make love" or "Let's fuck" loses (or wins).

National
Geographic
Game 80

For "National Geographic" you need a map detailing your favorite outdoor spots. Put the map up on a convenient wall. Then go to a designated spot on the map and make love in nature. When you return home, put a colored pin in that spot or draw a colored "X" on your map. See how vivid your map can become in this way as you record your sexual appreciation of nature.

Sex with Aliens
Game 81

One person is an alien from another planet who conveniently happens to have a humanoid body. The alien is interested in learning about sex but does not have a clue about how to do it. Fortunately they are a good student. You patiently and carefully instruct the alien in exactly what to do in various love-making techniques.

Stuffer
Game 82

For "Stuffer" one partner must start with a soft penis. Should your lover's penis suddenly become hard, you must go on to other games. Take the soft penis and stuff it into a soft, warm body space, such as a vagina. Experience the fun things that can be done with a soft penis. For example, you can use the soft penis as a magic wand to deliciously rap your partner's erotic sensitivities with little love taps. Use your fingers to push the penis into the folds of your partner's genitals. Also have your lover use their fingers to push the penis in and around where it feels best for them. Notice that the sensitivity of the penis is not directly related to how erect it might happen to be at any one time.

Oops!
Game 83

The male partner acts like he is a very inept or inexperienced lover. After intercourse begins, he lets his penis fall out of his lover. Then the players get to experience the thrill of insertion and penetration again, and again, and again.

Sex Talk
Game 84

Begin "Sex Talk" by making love to your partner in whatever way is most comfortable and familiar for you. While you are involved in your favorite love play, talk to your partner in a way that you would like them to talk to you when you are making love. The next time you and your partner make love, your partner then speaks to you in a manner which exactly reflects the way that you talked to them in the last session. Then it is the other person's turn to talk sexy in the manner they would like to hear it. What you say is what you will hear later, so do not censor yourself or be self-conscious that your love talk is either too romantic and sentimental, if that is what you like, or too earthy and explicit, if you enjoy that. It may take lots of practice to get this game down exactly right, so set aside lots of warm, juicy, exciting love play times for this game.

Lips and Balls
Game 85

Select one person to go first. Assist your lover in taking off all of their clothes and then have them lie down in a comfortable position. Blindfold your partner. The blindfolded person must remain in a receiving position for the duration of the game. Agree on a time frame for this game, but allow for at least a half-hour. Begin by lightly stroking your lover from head to toe. Kiss and lick the lucky receiver on the top part of their bodies. Skip over the genitals and kiss their feet and legs. Then slowly migrate up to their genital region.

If the receiving person is a male, you may orally stimulate your lover in any ways that you wish, but you must avoid putting his penis into your mouth. Start with your lover's scrotum and testicles. Tease the perineum with light finger strokes and with your tongue (see #20, "Chin Rest"). Kiss and lick underneath the testicles. Unlike penises, testicles may be taken lightly into the mouth and sucked on.

When you get to your lover's penis, kiss and lick it all over. Take the penis and rub your lips over the shaft like you were playing a harmonica.

If the receiving partner is a woman, begin in the same fashion with taking off your lover's clothes and having her lie down. After blindfolding your partner, begin by stroking and kissing your lover's body from head to foot circumscribing but not directly touching the genitals. Make your way slowly up to the temple of Venus. The active partner is to avoid contact with the clitoris during the agreed on time frame of this game. Also, they are to avoid putting their tongues or fingers directly into the vagina. All other genital areas are to be explored starting with the perineum and working up to include both the outer and inner lips.

When the agreed on time frame has expired, go on to other games.

One player picks an animal that they like. Then, for the duration of the game, you and your partner become that animal and enjoy sex the way that creature does. Favorite animals to be might include dolphins, whales, giraffes, dogs, cats, horses, or eagles.

Sex Animals
Game 86

Place a microphone or cassette recorder near your bed. Then proceed to make wonderful, glorious love with your partner. Express yourselves freely with spontaneous sounds of delight and ecstatic rapture. Use your recordings to remind yourself of your lover when you are apart, and also to play back when you are in bed together so that you can have stereophonic and quadraphonic echoes of your lovemaking. Use your recordings to get yourselves back in the mood, to reminisce about past tender moments, or to have group sex with just two people when you play your recording while you are making love. Keep a tape to play in your car when you are on the way home or stuck in traffic.

Sounds of Love
Game 87

See Game #60. This game is what a modern Tarzan and Jane do if they do not have a swimming pool or if it's a rainy day. In this game Tarzan and Jane make love in the bathtub.

If the water is not a sufficient lubricant, use a petroleum based lubricant. These petroleum based lubricants cannot be used with condoms.

Indoor T. and J.
Game 88

Select an active person for this game. The active partner narrates and describes love play in as graphic and detailed a way as possible. All four-letter words, Anglo-Saxon terms, and vernacular expressions are to be used in the description. The person playing the narrating

Talk Dirty to Me
Game 89

role begins the game by describing their own sexual feelings as arousal builds and as they see their lover's body responding to what is happening between them. Continue to narrate in this fashion throughout the course of your sex play. The other partner is an entranced listener in the beginning of this game, but may engage in a dirty dialogue in response to the narrator's speech, if moved to do so.

Kama Sutra
Game 90

Together you and your partner read the *Kama Sutra* or some other book of sexual technique. Then you try out one new thing that you read about that you have never done before, or perhaps never tried before in quite the way it is described in the book. Play this game over a time frame that includes several opportunities for love play.

Keep Away
Game 91

In "Keep Away" the male partner plays the active role. Begin the game by slowly arousing your partner's full erotic response in your most favorite ways. Then, when intercourse seems appropriate, tantalize your lover's genitals with the penis as if you were clumsily trying to insert it but do not know quite how to do it. Experience how exquisite it feels to have the penis playing around the entrance to the temple without actually going inside. Continue this game as long as you like and then go on to other games.

You and your lover plan a trip somewhere away from your home town. Maybe you go camping or sight-seeing or just for a drive into the country. Wherever you go, you make plans to stay at a comfortable motel or hotel somewhere on your route for at least one night. You celebrate your day of fun and new adventures with a wonderful night of love-making in your new surroundings.

If it is inconvenient for you to go out of town, plan to stay at a "no-tell motel" in your home town. You might pretend that you are having a secret affair with your lover.

Road Trip
Game 92

One partner is selected to be the teacher. This person then instructs their lover in how they masturbate themselves. This is a show and tell game. Demonstrate what feels good to you and then have your partner imitate this motion on you. Give lots of feedback to your partner and keep them practicing until they master the techniques that you like the most. Then the roles are reversed.

The Master in the Bay of Shun
Game 93

You agree to tell your partner one sexual fantasy every other day for an agreed upon period of time. The next day your lover must reciprocate by telling you a fantasy. If you are unable to see each other every day, play this game whenever you know you will be together. Fantasies can be as elaborate or as simple as you wish.

A Fantasy a Day
Game 94

Keeps
Game 95

The object of "Keeps" is to maintain a physical oneness of your two bodies in intercourse for as long as you can. Pace your physical movements to maintain just enough excitement and arousal so that you can stay genitally connected for as long as possible.

Picture Window
Game 96

Drive with your beloved to an overlook with a beautiful view. You might want to arrive just before sunset and watch the sun go down. Anticipate your wonderful moment together as it slowly gets dark. After it gets completely dark, get back in your car and make love in the car with the overlook as your picture window.

Rowboat
Game 97

There is something irresistibly romantic about gliding on a lake with your beloved in a rowboat or down the river in a canoe. Take your picnic supplies along so that you can have a picnic on a convenient shore after enjoying the sun and the water. Wear comfortable clothes suitable for outdoor lovemaking. Bring along your outdoor blanket and enjoy your picnic and then each other. (See also Game #62, "Picnic.")

Dear Diary
Game 98

Keep a diary of your sexual exploits. Have one partner record in graphic detail what you do together. Then, at quiet moments together, read what is in the diary. Make the diary fanciful or humorous rather than an actual record, if that is what you desire.

Surrender
Game 99

In "Surrender" the goal is to make one partner a total receiver while the other person is in an active and directing role. Select the more assertive partner to be the receiver in this game. The directing partner arouses, titillates, and makes love to the receiving partner while that person just receives, but does not do anything at all of an assertive nature.

The partner in the surrendering mode is undressed by their lover to begin this game. Then the receiver lies down in a comfortable position on their back while the active partner arouses and stimulates them. The receiver may reciprocate anything begun by the directing person but is not to initiate anything on their own. For example, the active partner may kiss or hug the receiver, who then may kiss and hug their lover in return. Should intercourse occur, the receiving partner participates fully in body motions, but does not change positions until requested to move by the initiator.

Wheel of Fortune Game 100

This game is called "Wheel of Fortune" because, after you and your partner agree to play one of the games, you do not know which one it is going to be. Use a calculator for this game. Tap out a full row of any numbers so that the entire display of the calculator is taken up with numbers. Hit the divide button, then do another full row of numbers, and push equals. Unless you are making love with Rainman, neither you nor your partner will be able to determine what numbers result from this random division.

If the number on the extreme left is an odd number, you have landed in the first set of games, numbers 1 through 99. If an even number comes up, you are in the second set of games, numbers 101-150. Then look at the last two numbers on the extreme right of the field. This tells you which game you and your lover will now play. If you get 00, this will be game 100 and you start over.

You can also use the square root key after you have entered a full field of numbers to determine which game it will be, if your calculator has one. If you are in the second field of games and get a number higher than 50, just start over to produce another random number until you get a number on the extreme right which is 50 or less.

Another method of playing this game is to write numbers from 1 to 150 on slips of paper. Fold them up and put them in a jar. Then when you want to select a random game, have one of you pull a numbered slip from the jar.

If you or your partner do not like the game that comes up randomly, just play again until you find one that you do enjoy.

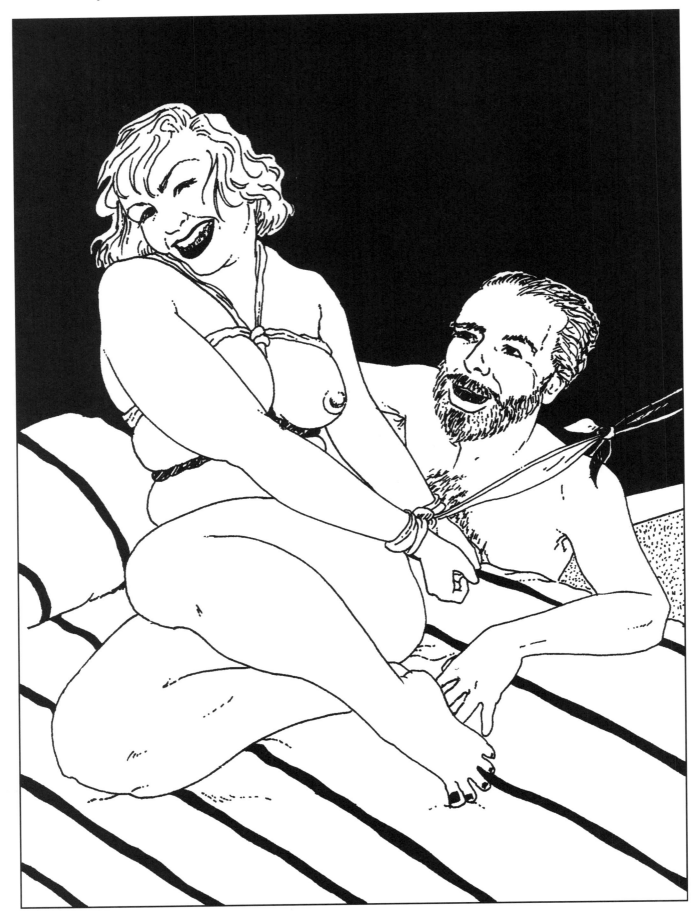

Restraint
Game 101

In "Restraint" the goal is to experience a heightened sensation through having part of your body lightly restrained. Always use soft materials for restraints and never tie any body parts very tight. If sensation is lost in a body part, this is definitely too tight and the restraints should be removed and adjusted. Neckties, ace bandages, and panty hose work well and are recommended for novice restrainers and restrainees.

Remember that the game alteration and game termination code words apply to this game. Once your lover is comfortably restrained, proceed to other games in which one partner is in a totally receiving role. (See #102, "Torture of Delight.")

Torture of Delight
Game 102

Decide which partner is going to be the receiver. This person is then restrained by their lover using soft restraints of some kind. (See #101, "Restraint," for details.) The active partner then proceeds to "torture" their victim by arousing them while they are unable to do anything but receive.

Begin by lightly touching and stroking your lucky victim from head to toe. Take your time and use very light gentle strokes. Then kiss and lick all of your lover's body from top to bottom. Use your hair and the top of your head to sensuously nuzzle your partner again from head to toe. With each pass over the body, you also stroke, kiss, lick, and nuzzle the genitals but only on the way to other parts of the body. After you have lightly stroked, kissed, licked, and nuzzled your lover from top to bottom, focus your attention on the genitals. At this point you may choose to end the game, move on to another game (see games #45, #69, #103, #115, and #131), or switch and let the other partner be the receiver.

Toys and Us
Game 103

One partner is selected to be the receiver. The receiving person is blindfolded and then restrained on a massage table or bed on either their stomach or their back, whichever they prefer. (See #101, "Restraint," for details of how best to do this.) The active partner then proceeds to lightly stroke their lover's body from head to foot leaving no part of the body untouched.

At this point the initiating partner opens a secret briefcase full of love toys that they have painstakingly collected and prepared for just this game. Inside are a variety of different implements of sensation. These include various kitchen accessories, strips of leather, beads, feathers, brushes, pieces of various kinds of fabric including silk and suede, lengths of knotted string, paddles, whips, riding crops, small sticks, hollow tubes made out of different kinds of materials, various furry objects, and a dildo made out of silicon.

The object of this game is to give your lover a wonderfully sensuous experience of the distinct feeling of these items on different parts of their body. If you are the active person in this game, try out the various implements on your own skin first to get an idea of how it feels and also to discover what intensity is created by various kinds of strokes on the body with the items.

The receiving person is to give the toy master feedback about how the objects feel on their body. Yellow means, "This is too painful or too intense." Red states, "I do not like the way that object feels at all. Stop with that one." Green means, "I really like that one, keep doing it." Purple signifies, "I like that one, but more intensity please." Be sure to give attention to both sides of your lover's body.

The hollow tubes are for dramatic effect. If the tubes are made of a light material, striking the body with them will create a lot of noise but very little sensation. Use the knotted strings to pull around your lover's genitals and between their legs. Slowly pull the string either around your partner's penis and testicles or through her labia.

If you are going to use whips, try to find some that are made of very soft material. Elkhide whips, for example, are very soft. You can make your own whip using pieces of cut up suede or bicycle inner tubes. Whip use requires some practice and skill since the whip ends will sometimes wrap around a body and hit where you are not aiming.

Paddles can feel good if you use relatively light strokes and have a paddle made out of a padded or soft material. Ping-pong paddles coated with rubber work fairly well.

Whenever experimenting with a new toy, start off very lightly and gently and work up to more intensity if desired, as you request and receive feedback from your partner about how it feels.

Avoid any kind of striking blows to the vulnerable areas of the body at all times. These include the neck, face, and head areas, kidneys, spine, joints, hands, feet, breasts, ribs, stomach, and abdomen.

In this game you proceed as in "Sounds of Love" (Game #87), but this time you really ham it up for the sake of the recording. You and your partner make really exaggerated noises in a humorous parody of pornographic sound tracks.

Outrageous Sounds of Love Game 104

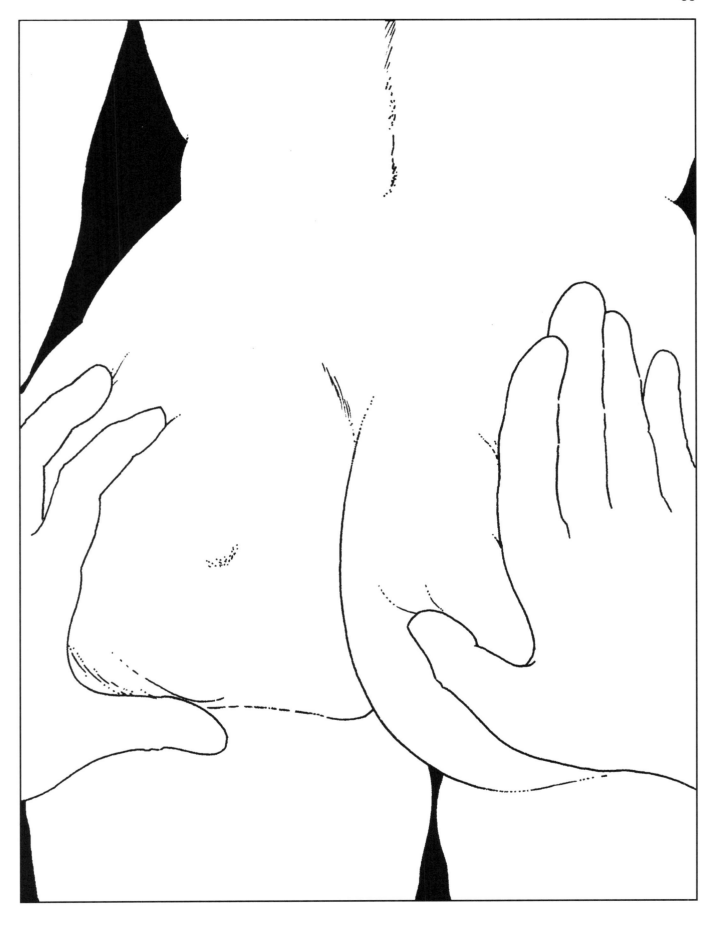

In "Rubbum" one person is selected to be the receiver, and the other person is then the active partner. The initiating partner tenderly undresses their beloved and has them lie down in a comfortable position on their front side. Then, using scented massage oil, the active partner beings to give the receiver a wonderful massage.

Begin by sitting astride your lover's buns (avoid sitting directly on the buttocks) and massage the neck, shoulders, and along the side of the spine. Then work on the feet. (Consult a massage book if you are unsure how to work with these areas of your partner's body.) Then the initiator begins to massage their lover's bum. Begin by placing one hand on your partner's buttocks and one hand on the side of their neck. Then grab handfuls of your lover's bum and gently squeeze them. Place your palms on your partner's buns and, keeping one cheek still, rotate the other cheek. Then switch cheeks and rotate the other cheek. Then rotate both cheeks in opposite directions, and change the direction and rotate the other way. Place your palm directly over the end of the spine and rotate the entire buttocks area.

Starting from the side of your lover, reach around as far as you can and pull your hands over their bum, pulling first one hand, and then following it with the other hand in a pullover motion. When you get to the division between the buns and the legs, pull your hands over from the side through this crevice several times. With your hands on each side of your partner, move the hands up toward the spine squeezing the buns together. Then slide your hands down the bum towards the feet and repeat the motion several times.

Put the palm of your hand on the division of the cheek and the leg and push up parallel to the crease in your lover's bum. Then push up the other side in the same way. Turn facing your lover's feet and pull up toward you on the side of each cheek. You can use a lot of pressure on the last two strokes.

Rubbum
Game 105

Spread your partner's cheeks and run your hand down the crevice from the upper part of the buns ending at the leg. Then stroke the other crevice. Outline the triangular bony structure at the end of the spine with your fingers. With your palms on each side of the spine, move out to the sides of the body just above the buttocks.

Trace the spine down to its very end and very gently massage underneath the very end of the tail bone. (This might be a sensitive area on your partner, so be sure to check in with them about how this feels.) Start at your lover's neck and, putting your index finger on one side of the spine and your middle finger on the other side, slowly pull your hand down your partner's back along all the length of their spine. With each stroke move a little further down the spine. When you get to the end of the spine, spill over and massage down the crevice of the buns. (Do not massage from the anus to the vagina, however.) Repeat this last stroke several times. Work your way back up to the neck by placing one thumb on each side of the spine and slowly walk your way back up to the neck.

Scratch your sweetie's bum lightly. As a final stroke lightly slap your lover's buns with your hands. The receiving partner must make no active moves during the entirety of this game, but they give continuous feedback to their lover about how each stroke feels.

Unveiling
Game 106

In "Unveiling" one partner is blindfolded and becomes the receiver for the duration of the game. Begin by slowly undressing your lover one piece of clothing at a time. As each piece of clothing is removed, stop and slowly appreciate this view of your beloved before going on. Really drink in the full visual magnificence of the revealed part of your lover's body. Then move your face close to your beloved to fully experience the wonderful natural aroma. Finally, gently and lovingly caress the exposed part with your fingers, and then smother it with kisses and licks. Once your partner is completely nude, go on to other games.

Riskee
Game 107

It is very important that each partner receive a turn. Decide who goes first. Then this person shares a sexual secret with their lover that they have never shared with them before, and perhaps have never shared with anyone at all. An example of a secret would be some particular sensual experience that is erotic for you, but not for everyone, such as enjoying licking someone's armpits.

Ying-Yang
Game 108

For "Yin-Yang" decide which partner is going to go first. This person then begins to initiate love play and to direct everything that is happening by giving specific and explicit instruction of what their lover is to do at every point. ("Kiss me on my neck now. A little harder.") Then, at unpredictable times, the active partner suddenly says "switch!" This is a signal for their partner to take over direction of the love play. The person who began initiating does not do anything at this point until their partner instructs them to do something. Then their lover takes over direction until they say switch. In this way the direction and control of the sex play is passed from partner to partner throughout the duration of the game.

Peaking Allowed
Game 109

Some lovers enjoy intensifying their most passionate moments by having their partner give them a peak stimulus at just the right moment. In this game the object is to give your lover a sexual peak using either slapping on the buttocks, or pinching of the nipples. The person who is to receive directs the peak stimulus. Whenever the receiving partner is at just the right moment of arousal, he or she says "now." (Use another cue if you like.) This is the signal for their lover to slap their buns or pinch their nipples. Start off with relatively gentle slaps or pinches and let your partner give you a cue for more intensity, if it is desired. Use "yellow" to tell them to lighten the intensity, and "red" to mean stop completely. "Green" would be a request to continue, and "purple" would ask for more intensity.

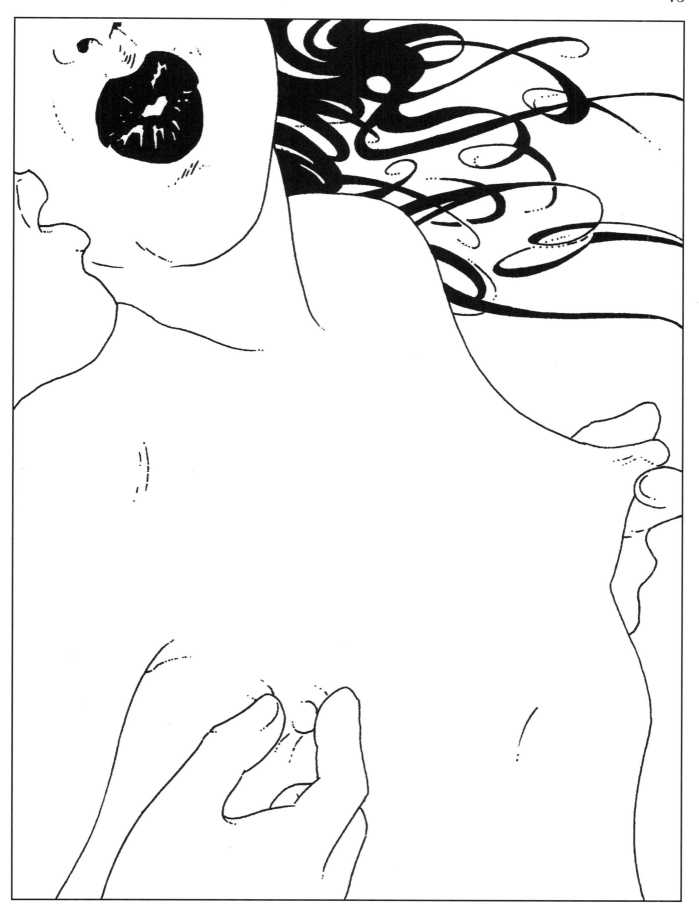

Select one partner to be the active person and their lover is then the receiver. Have the receiver lie face down in a comfortable full reclining position.

Begin by massaging your lover's back and particularly their buns (see Game #105, "Rubbum," for details on this). Spread your partner's legs and drip warm massage oil down the crack of their bum. Taking your index finger, trace a line from the end of the spine downward. Go around the anus when you get to this erotic zone of your beloved. Stroke the crevice of the cheek from the top of the buns to the leg, and again avoid the anus. Place your thumbs on each side of your lover's anus and gently pull it apart, squeeze it together, pull it apart, squeeze it together, and so on.

For the next portion of this game if you are the active partner, be sure that your finger nails are trimmed and that you have no nicks or cuts on your fingers. Use finger cots if desired for hygiene or safe sex considerations. Never insert a finger into the vagina that has been in the anus without washing it first.

Pour some oil directly into your partner's love dimple. Then using just the tip of your finger, lightly stroke your partner's anus. Leisurely allow your finger to sink into your lover's anal opening as they relax and let you in. Use an extremely slow pace for insertion of the finger. Use circular strokes around the rim of your partner's anus rather than rapid in and out strokes. When you have gone beyond the anal sphincter, very slowly pull your finger out. Feel the anal sphincter grab at your finger on the way out. Then, just before it falls out, reinsert the finger slowly as before and repeat the slow withdrawal several times.

Check with your lover each time you do a different movement or stroke and see whether it is completely comfortable for them. Encourage your partner to give you their ideas about other kinds of stimulation they would like in this area of their bodies as well as continuous feedback about how each stroke feels for them.

The Finger That Came in From the Cold Game 110

Wishes
Game 111

One partner plays the role of the Fairy Goddess or the Magical Prince, and their lover is the lucky human who has done something which puts them in the good graces of this magical being. The Goddess/Prince says to the mortal, "Now, I will grant you one wish." That person then states a wish which involves some aspect of love play. (No fair asking for a new refrigerator.) The Goddess/Prince always grants the wish.

If you are playing the role of the Goddess/Prince and your human asks you to do something with which you do not feel comfortable, find a way to grant their wish anyway by doing something which approximates the wish. For example, if the human wants you to do cunnilingus or fellatio and you do not feel comfortable with this, kiss on and around your partner's genitals, between their legs, the area between the genitals and the anus, etc. Always find some way that you can make your human's wish come true, even if it involves an approximation of the exact request. Be sure that you both take turns playing the wisher in this game.

The Iceman
Cometh
Game 112

One partner is selected to be the receiver and is blindfolded by their lover. The active partner slowly and deliberately undresses their lover and assists them in lying in a comfortable reclining position on their back.

Then the active person takes a wet towel and slowly pulls it over various parts of their lover's body. Turning to a bucket of ice cubes which is conveniently secreted near the blindfolded partner, the "iceman" takes an ice cube and applies it with masterful sensitivity to particular areas of their lover's body. An ice cube is taken into the hand by the "iceman" and held over their lover's body so that drops of cold water fall deliciously onto their partner.

Hulk Hogan and Henrietta
Game 113

Imagine how the wrestling hero Hulk Hogan might make love. (He probably does not do it this way, but it is a good image to stimulate the mind.) Decide who will play Hulk. Either partner will do. Then proceed with your love play in whatever fashion you desire. When you arrive at the point of intercourse, have the person playing Hulk be on top. He or she then proceeds to hold their partner down by the wrists as they make love, preventing them from making any active movements at all. The receiving partner uses the word "yellow" as a code word to mean, "Please be less intense with what you are doing," and "red" to mean "stop completely."

Love Wolves
Game 114

Wolves, dogs, and other animals engage in a lot of mild biting in their sex play. In this game you try to emulate these creatures by seeing how you can create pleasurable feelings by using your teeth on various sensitive areas of your lover's body. Be very careful in this game not to break the skin of your partner. Enjoy discovering what vulnerable areas of the body really respond well to a very carefully calibrated bite. Necks and shoulders, for example, secretly love gentle bites. Be careful not to leave bruise marks on your lover's skin, if this is not desired.

Chocolate Torture
Game 115

For "Chocolate Torture" the receiving partner is either restrained or agrees to remain in a totally receiving mode throughout the duration of the game no matter what sensations they may be feeling. However, the receiving partner must give their lover verbal feedback on what they are experiencing, either through words or through groans, moans, and sighs. Whenever the receiving partner stops with the feedback, the active person stops what they are doing as well.

The active partner takes some chocolate syrup and spreads a light coat over the entirety of their lover's genital area. If the receiving partner is male, be sure to include testicles, scrotum, perineum, and the underside of the penis. If the receiving person is female, cover the outer lips, the area between the inner and outer lips, the inner lips, and the perineum as well.

The active partner then proceeds to slowly lick off the chocolate syrup. Whenever the taste of chocolate is gone, the active person moves on to clean off another area until their lover is completely eaten off. Then, if you would like, put on another coat of chocolate and start all over again.

The Goose's
Revenge
Game 116

The male partner is either restrained or agrees not to move a muscle. The female partner arouses her lover using all of her skill. She then takes the man's erect penis in her hand and plays with it around her clitoris and the wonderful love folds of her body. She places it near the entrance to her vagina but doesn't let it go in, or lets it go in, but only a little. She uses the penis as a toy for her pleasure but always stops short of full insertion.

Be sure you have your partner's sincere consent before you play this game.

Your partner describes their meeting with a fantasy lover. By some miraculous, wondrous chance, a convenient opportunity arose to make love. They proceed to describe this delicious encounter with Robert Redford, Jamie Lee Curtis, Kevin Costner, Madonna, and others. As they describe the fulfillment of their delight with their fantasy person, their partner plays the role of the dream lover, doing exactly what the dream lover did in the fantasy.

"Do You Know Who I Saw at the Mall Today?" Game 117

The partners play whatever competitive games they normally play together as a couple such as scrabble, tennis, gin rummy, and so forth. The winner then gets to play the role they desire in any game of their choice in this book.

Games People Play Game 118

One player plays the role of a little boy or girl. The other person is the opposite gender parent. The little boy or girl has been naughty and the parent has to figure out some suitable punishment for them. An over-the-knees spanking might be appropriate, for example.

Bad Boy/Bad Girl Game 119

Outrageous Game 120

You think of some outrageous sexual adventure of which you have knowledge or which you made up. Your partner then says, "Oh, that is nothing. Did you hear about . . . ?" and goes on to narrate something even more scandalous. You take turns trying to top each other with ever more outrageous stories and accounts of the sexually bizarre. The things you relate do not have to be true or factual. Start with relatively normal things and slowly escalate into the outlandish and farfetched.

Lesbians Game 121

The lovers are two lesbians who make glorious and delicious love to each other. It helps if one of the partners has some actual experience with lesbian love play. If this is not the case, be sure to remember that neither lover has a penis.

Dresssing Strategically Game 122

You and your partner play your favorite board game, card game, or any other competitive sport or game where one of you is the clear winner. The winner then has won the right to dress or undress their lover in any fashion he or she chooses for an agreed on period of time. The winner may choose to dress their partner in unusual ways or to have them go about (in private or in public) missing some strategic part of clothing such as their underwear.

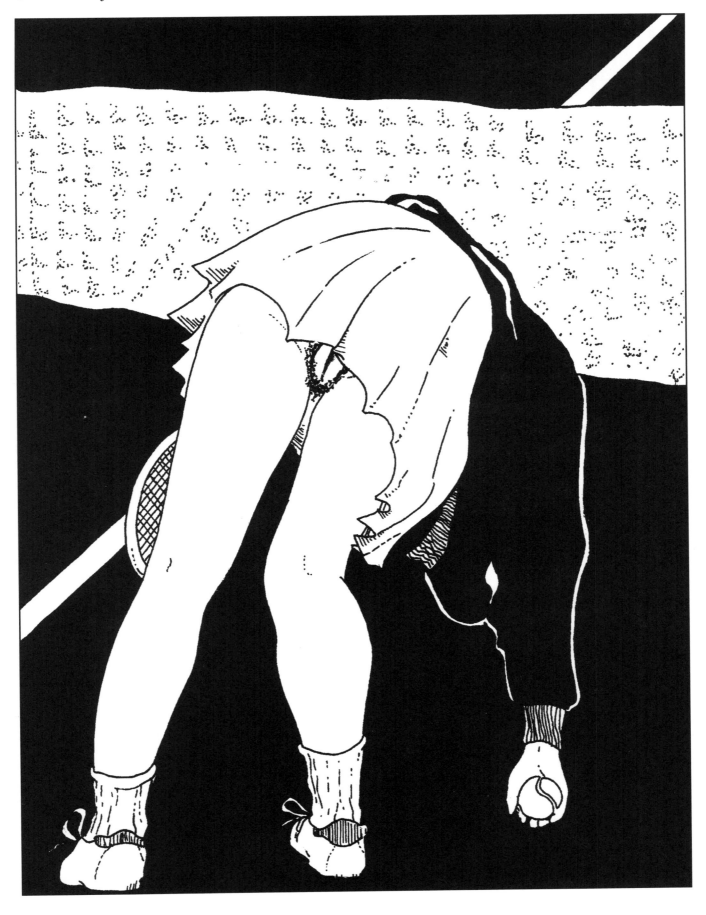

King and Queen
Game 123

(Also known as the Master and Slave Game.) Flip a coin to determine who is going to be the King or Queen and who is going to be the slave. The King or Queen then pretends that they are the Pharaoh of Egypt or someone equivalent in status. The other person is a slave who must do all of the King's or Queen's bidding, including attending to their very private person.

Hot Tub/Cold Pool
Game 124

If you have ever been to a hot springs you may have had occasion to go from the hot pool into the cold pool and then back again. This produces a very interesting sensual experience.

One person is selected to be the receiver. The active partner then restrains and blindfolds their lover. The initiator in this game uses a hot towel and a piece of cold metal, like a cold soda can, to give their lover alternate sensations of cold and hot.

If you want to go for something a little more intense, you might wish to try ice cubes for cold and a lighted candle for hot. The lighted candle is tipped over so that hot wax spills on their body, one drop at a time. Be sure not to use beeswax candles. They are too hot and can burn your partner. Paraffin candles on the other hand are relatively cool. Never hold the candle more than two feet above the body. Also, do not drip wax on any part of the face.

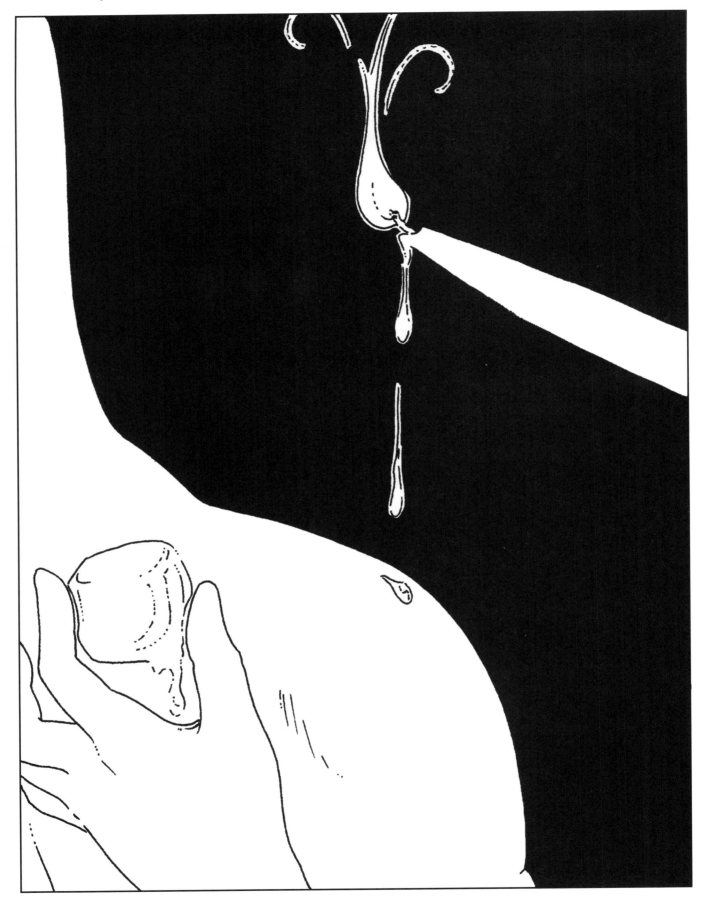

The Prodigal Finger
Game 125

In "Prodigal Finger" the male partner will be the receiver. Begin the game by playing "The Finger that Came in From the Cold," #110. This time let the finger go in deeper than before and search out the prostate. It will be located about two inches, or a little less, into the rectum. (Be sure your nails are trimmed for this game.) Turn your hand so that the palm is pointing toward your partner's belly button when you let your finger go into your partner. See if you can feel the prostate gland from inside your lover's body cavity. At this point apply pressure to that spot as you pleasure your partner with your other hand or your mouth. Be sure to get lots of feedback from your lover about what touch and pressure feels good to them on the prostate.

Body Servant
Game 126

Body servant is one way to play the King and Queen Game, #123. In this case the slave is the body servant of the royal personage. The body servant baths, dresses, and otherwise attends to all of the personal needs of the King or Queen.

Fantasy Creation
Game 127

The lovers create a sexual fantasy together by means of a sentence completion. The first person to go starts out with a suggestive scenario. "Once upon a time there was a young girl who was very . . . ." Their lover fills in the missing word and carries the story a little further, stopping in the middle of an interesting part, and letting the other person continue. After you finish your story, see if you can recreate some portion of the fantasy in your own love play.

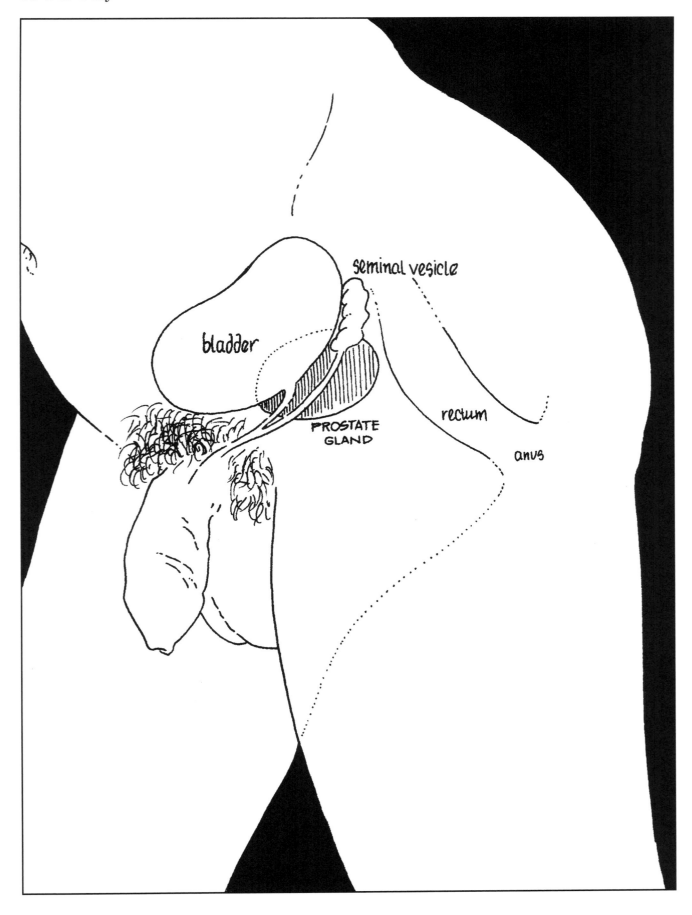

For Sake
Game 128

In this game you are to forsake your normal inhibitions about telling your partner the full truth about the experience of your love-making. This game is for the sake of your mutual love together.

Choose one person to go first. This person then takes two or three minutes to tell their partner how much they love and appreciate them and especially what a wonderfully sensitive and skillful sexual partner they are. Be specific about what it is that you really appreciate in your beloved (that they are willing to take the risk to play Game #107, "Riskee," with you, for example). Take a longer time if you wish to more fully shower your lover with verbal appreciations.

Then tell your partner one thing about your sex play together that does not work for you as well as you would like. Be careful not to blame your lover or make them feel wrong about what they are doing, but speak in terms of what *your* experience is when they are doing a particular sexual activity.

When the first person is complete, their partner gets a turn. After each of you has had a turn, decide if you want to continue the game or go on to other games.

Gays
Game 129

Both partners are gay males who celebrate their love for each other as only gay men can do. If you are a male-female couple, have the female partner really give herself over to the role play of being a man. Do not be concerned with whether what you do together is really what gay men do. (Your imaginings might be different from their reality.) Just enjoy the fantasy of being with a partner of the same gender or the role play of being a different gender.

Sex Researcher
Game 130

Both partners close their eyes and open Krafft-Ebing up to a random page (any book or magazine describing sexual variations will do). The person playing the role of the interviewer has now met someone who truly enjoys what is described on that page. The interviewee plays the role of someone who likes that activity and tries to make it sound convincing as a really fun and neat thing to do. The interviewer asks very specific and personal questions about the variation.

Wet and Hard
Game 131

Begin "Wet and Hard" by choosing one person to be the receiver. Restrain your lover using soft restraints (see #101, "Restraint," for details). The active partner then begins to gently arouse their lover using light touch, kissing, licking, and nuzzling. (See #102, "Torture of Delight.")

When your partner is really aroused, turn your attention to the genitals. The object of this game is to arouse your lover to the maximum possible extent but not allow them to come, or at least to postpone orgasm for as long as possible. Massage oil is a really good way to arouse your lover in this manner since it allows you to rub and stroke your partner vigorously while reducing friction.

Mesmerized
Game 132

One partner is picked as the active person and the other partner is the receiver. Decide on a time period for one person to be the active partner and then switch roles. For example, one partner might get to be the active partner for a week's time, or one day, or for part of a day.

During the agreed on time span, both lovers pretend that the active partner has given the receiving partner a powerful posthypnotic suggestion. Whenever the active partner says "mushroom," or your own pet word, the receiving partner undergoes a sudden and complete lapse of will. In fact, the receiving person just freezes in place until instructed to do something by their lover. The active partner then guides the mesmerized person through whatever it is that they want to do at that period of time. This could be a particular form of sexual play or just washing the dishes.

After the agreed on time period has elapsed, the person who was the receiver now plays the active role. Be sure that both partners get to play the active role in this game.

Hot Tales
Game 133

This is a good game to play with your partner if you happen to be geographically separated for any reason. If you are fortunate enough to be living together, you can still play the game. Write a scorching account of wild, passionate sexual play. The things you write about do not even have to be possible. Make it as fanciful as you like or as true to real life as you wish. You can include your partner or yourself in the stories if you want. When you have finished a good sexual story, put it in an envelope and mail it to your lover. Try to disguise the source by using a standardized mailing label or typing the label and using no return address. Then mail it to your own address so that your lover is totally surprised to hear from you. Take turns being the writer and the receiver.

Conjunction
Game 134

The object of "Conjunction" is to have a simultaneous orgasm with your partner. You and your lover stimulate yourselves through masturbation. The first person to get close to the peak of the mountain waits until their lover catches up. Then you both try to hit the summit at the same moment.

Give your partner clear signals about how close you are. One way to do this is to use a number code. Five would signal when you are really starting to get turned on. Nine would mean you had reached that plateau just before you come. When both partners reach nine, then you coordinate by using 9.5, and so forth, until you both reach 10.

Good Genie
Game 135

You rub your partner the right way and behold the Good Genie appears, ready to grant you three wishes. You and your lover have already decided beforehand which one is going to play the Genie in the following way: either play Game #118, "Games People Play," or add up the letters in your first and last name (maiden name, if married). The one who has the most number of letters in both names combined is the Genie.

The person lucky enough to have summoned the Genie then makes three specific requests of their partner. This could be asking to play three separate sexual games from this book, or it could be asking for three distinct kinds of sexual intimacies, strokes, attentions, etc. It could be making love at three specific times of your own choice, and so forth. The only restriction on the requests is that they have to involve a dimension of love play.

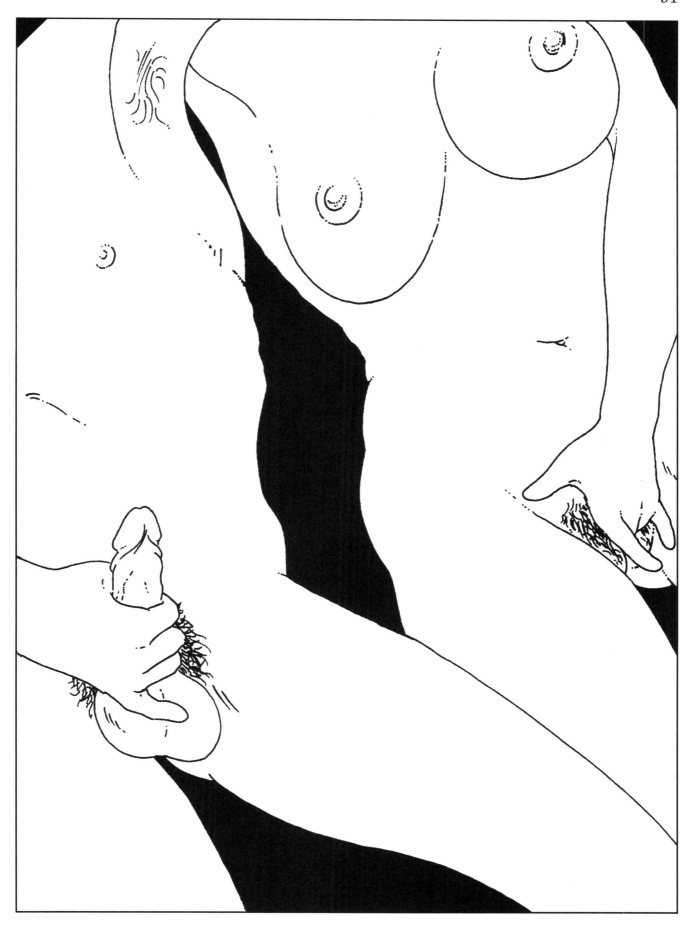

"Pornographic Movie" is similar to "Home Video," #64. This time you and your partner pretend that you are making a pornographic movie using your home video equipment. Ham it up as much as possible for the camera and have fun later seeing how outrageous you look as you imitate famous sexual movie stars.

Pornographic Movie Game 136

"Hello Yellow" is to be played in the shower with your lover. You begin by fervently taking off each other's clothes and kissing and hugging. You are in such a hurry to get into the shower that you do not pause to urinate before going into the waters. No problem. Release your golden flood onto some part of your partner's body, such as their feet or leg, and enjoy the warm rush.

Hello Yellow Game 137

This is an exhibitionism and voyeurism game. Only in this case, the two people involved are you and your lover. Wear something very revealing that your partner has picked out for you or that you have decided on in collaboration. Then very discreetly, so that no one else knows what is going on, expose yourself to your lover. You might want to do this at home, for example, or in your car when you are driving on an uncrowded road, or in a restaurant where no one else can see.

E. and V. Game 138

Select one of the partners to play the active role. This lover will assume various demeanors in your sex play for the next three or four times that you are together. He/she might be bossy and demanding in one demeanor, then submissive and meek in the next. Vary your demeanors using different extremes from intensely personal and romantic to impersonal and nameless, from whorish to Victorian, or from serious to humorous, for example. Have fun inventing new demeanors to surprise your lover. Should any of the demeanors not work at all for your partner, they may say the code word to end the role play at any time.

Demeanors
Game 139

Hopefully this game will result in a lot of giggling as well as figgling. Begin by seducing your partner in whatever way has worked best for you in the past. Once you are into a love-making mode, proceed from your favorite forms of foreplay to intercourse, but do not be in any hurry to get to that point. Really indulge yourself in the wonderful feelings of penetrating and being penetrated by your lover. Then stop stroking before the male partner reaches climax.

Remain connected for a few tender moments, and then allow your lover's penis to get soft. Then begin with foreplay again. Once a good state of arousal is reached, go on to penetration once more. The second penetration will count as the second round. See if you can last through five rounds of foreplay and intercourse without the male partner having an orgasm. Should an orgasm result in spite of your most conscientious efforts, keep playing the game and see if you can continue for a while after climax. Keep the giggle in your figgle. Do not take this game too seriously.

Figgle and Giggle
Game 140

Simon Says
Game 141

One of you is selected as the initiator and the other partner carefully and completely follows their lover's lead throughout the game. The initiator can begin any form of love play that they like whenever they wish. The person playing the follower role asks the initiator to be explicit about what it is that they want to do. If the initiator begins by saying that they want to make love, their partner must respond to this request by asking, "How do you want to make love?" The follower then does exactly what the initiator requests, as the initiator guides the love play in a step by step fashion. The follower always asks for explicit instructions at each point and does only what the initiator tells them to do, but no more and no less.

Pincher
Game 142

Sometimes it feels good to have parts of the body pinched as long as this is done with exactly the right degree of intensity. Nipples, for example, frequently like to be pinched by a really knowledgeable nipple tweaker. One partner is selected to be the tweaker, and the other person is then the tweakee.

A color code can be used to communicate the degree of pleasant or unpleasant sensations. Green might indicate, for instance, that more intensity was needed, and blue could signify an intermediate pleasantness, but still not the best. Purple would mean that just the right amount of intensity had been reached. Yellow, orange, and red would indicate an increasing range of discomfort.

Sensitivity of breasts and nipples, as well as other body areas, can vary a lot from day to day, particularly in female partners. Sensitivity may also vary considerably depending on the degree of arousal of your partner. See also Game #146, "Titillation."

The Electric Lover
Game 143

The human body is really a field of energy. Often, however, we are not fully aware of the energy components of our own and our lover's body. In this game begin by sitting on the floor with your legs wrapped around each other and arms around your partner's back. Have the taller person on top. Synchronize your breathing so that you are both breathing in exactly the same rhythm.

Then together you and your lover visualize a movement of energy in your bodies. Starting from the crown of one partner's head, visualize the energy flowing down to the soles of that partner's feet, then into the other person's feet, and up through the crown of their head, and then across to the other partner's head.

After experiencing this closed energy circuit through your bodies, have one partner take their hands and lightly touch their partner's body trying to feel directly the energy field around their lover. You may move your hands slightly above your partner's body and feel the energy field there as it extends outward from the body. (Use this game as a warm-up for Game #145, "Hyperventilation.")

♥ ♥ ♥

Spanker
Game 144

Spanking of the buttocks can feel good if it is done with just the right amount of intensity. One partner is selected to be the receiver. The active partner positions their lover in a very comfortable position such as across their knees or lying on the edge of the bed.

Spanking is very light at first and then gradually increases in intensity as the receiver gives color code feedback about how pleasurable it feels. Green will mean, "too light, harder please." Blue will be an intermediate level of intensity and purple just the right amount. Yellow, orange, and red will indicate a scale of increasing discomfort.

It generally works best for this game to space out strokes rather than having a rapid succession of them. This allows the receiver to fully absorb and experience each stroke before another sensation arrives. You might throw in an unexpectedly rapid succession of spanks for an occasional surprise though. Experiment with alternating moderately intense strokes and very light stroking of the buttocks with finger touch. A strong stroke sensitizes the whole area, and then very light touch suddenly becomes very prominent and sensual. Try to avoid spanking too much in any one spot.

The most sensitive and erotic spots are generally described by the areas immediately above and to the sides of the crease of the buns and then around the bottom of the bum just above where the buttocks intersect with the legs.

Hyperventilation Game 145

For "Hyperventilation" the partners assume a comfortable intimate posture together such as the leg straddle posture where both partner's legs are wrapped around their lover's waist, with the taller person's legs on top. Begin by making eye contact with your beloved and breathe at your normal pace for a while as you put your breath into rhythm with your lover's breathing. Then slowly one of you begins to accelerate the pace of your breathing while your partner matches you breath for breath. Soon you are both breathing more quickly and deeply than usual. If you feel uncomfortable with the rapid breathing, slowly decelerate to the usual pace and then breathe rapidly again together if you wish.

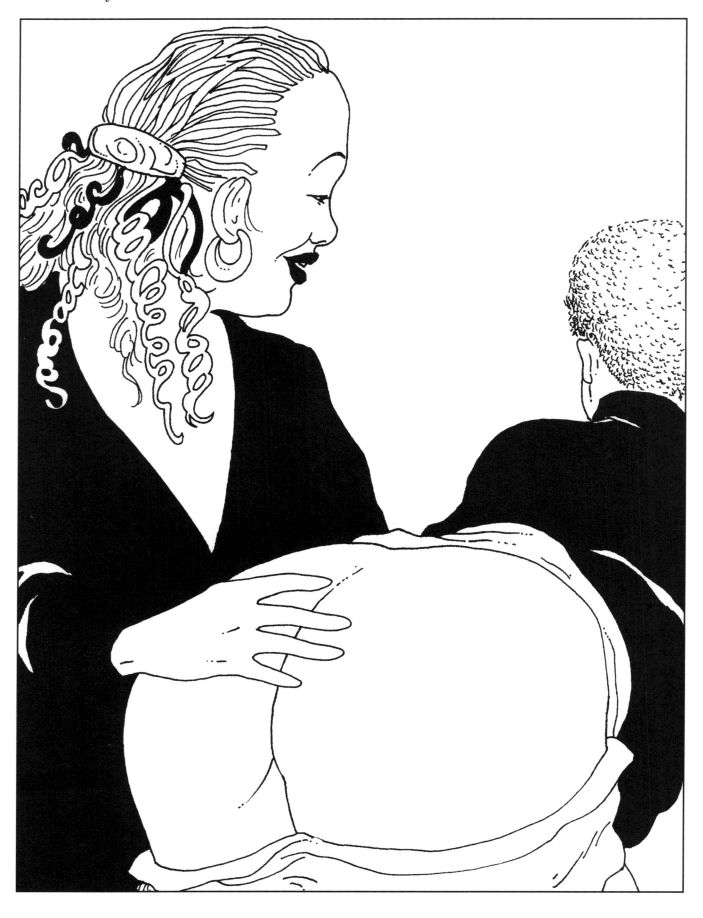

Titillation
Game 146

In "Titillation" the nipples are the focus of your attention. Decide which partner goes first. The active person will then blindfold their partner after slowly and gently undressing them.

"Titillation" can be played in conjunction with #142, "Pincher." The purpose of this game is to titillate your lover's nipples in as many sensuous and erotic ways as you can possibly imagine. The blindfolded person then gives feedback to their partner about the effectiveness of the various techniques. Use a 10 point scale with 0 being "I cannot feel anything," to 10 being "WOW!" If something is wow and then another sensation is even better, use 11 or more. If something is unpleasant or causes discomfort, use minus numbers proportional to the degree of the discomfort.

Begin by lightly stroking your partner's nipples. Then begin kissing and sucking. Try to pay attention to which of the variations you use to orally stimulate your lover are the most effective (licking the nipple, hard sucking, light sucking, pulling the nipple up with your lips, encircling the nipple with the tongue, batting the nipple back and forth with the tongue, etc.). Pay attention to see if one nipple is more sensitive than the other using the different strokes.

Coordinate light genital stroking with your nipple stroking and see what results. Experiment with exciting the nipple with other body parts (the face, hair, penis, nose, teeth, testicles, etc.). Also play with stimulating the area surrounding the nipple and behind the breast button. See what result you get by applying ice to the nipple. Also try various very soft instruments such as feathers, make-up brushes, soft strings and cords, pipe cleaners, and so forth.

Each partner gets a turn receiving in this game. Be aware that female receivers may have a very wide fluctuation of nipple and breast sensitivity at various times of their menstrual cycle.

Take Away
Game 147

Play a card game like gin rummy. Any two-handed card game will do. The loser then has one item of clothing taken away from them by the winner. (Both partners must start with the same number of items on.) Whoever is left with any clothing on when one of the partner's is completely nude is the winner. The winner then has magical power over the loser, being able to command them to do anything they wish. No fair asking your partner to paint the house. The loser must then do whatever the winner commands them to do.

Ask Mr. Head/Ask
Virginia
Game 148

Rather than talking directly to your partner and using their name, you address yourself totally to their genitals to which they have given a proper name (Mr. Head, Penasaurus, Buddy, etc. or Virginia, Flo, Miss Pussy, etc.). One partner asks Mr. Head a question like, "What is your pleasure today, Mr. Head?" Mr. Head responds by saying, "I think I would like to be tickled," or "I would really like to visit Virginia today. Do you think she might be at home?" At this point Virginia will have to answer for herself with regard to whether she is entertaining visitors or not. Carry on conversations in this way between your nether neighbors and discover what it is that they like the most and what they are in the mood for on that particular day.

Indentured Servant Game 149

An indentured servant is someone who has obligated themselves to serve someone else for a contracted period of time. Determine who goes first in the following way. Take a calculator and tap out a series of numbers until all of the field is taken up with as many numbers as it will hold. Then push the division key, punch in another full field of numbers, and hit equals. If the number on the far right hand side of the display is an even number, the female partner wins. If it is an odd number, the male partner wins. (If you have another gender configuration, decide who is going to be the odd and who the even player.) Then look at the last two numbers on the right. This is the number of minutes you are now sexually indentured to your lover to participate in any sexual activity they desire for the period of time that comes up.

The indentured partner still can end the game or request that their partner change the instructions by using their game termination code word or the game modification code word.

Invent a Game Game 150

Here is a short list of more wonderfully sexy games. The only things lacking are the instructions. Make up your own rules and enjoy the game.

Underwear
Seduction
Puppy Dog
Kitten
Perversion
Housewife's Revenge
The Sexiest Woman/Man in the World Just
    Did . . .
Wine Taster of People
Naughty Nurse
Turn Back the Clock

AFTERWORD

I hope you fully enjoyed the 150 sex games. I want to hear from you. Let me know what worked for you and what did not. I would appreciate any constructive feedback that you may have.

Do you have an idea of your own for a game? Your suggestions about future games for an advanced version of *For Play* will be invaluable. You may contact either the author or the illustrator of *For Play* by writing to Waterfall Press, 5337 College Avenue, Suite 139, Oakland, California 94618.

ABOUT THE AUTHOR

Walter A. Shelburne, Ph.D., lives in Oakland, California where he writes and works as a personal consultant doing personal channeling and philosophical counseling. Walter is the author of *Mythos and Logos in the Thought of Carl Jung: The Theory of the Collective Unconscious in Scientific Perspective* published by the State University of New York Press in 1988. *For Play* originated as a result of his research into the philosophy of sex and love. He is currently working on another book in this area to be called *A Thinking Person's Guide to Sex and Love.*

ABOUT THE ILLUSTRATOR

Molly Kiely is a young Canadian artist who lives in San Francisco. Molly graduated from the Fine Art Department of the University of Waterloo, Canada and currently works as an underground cartoonist. Her most recent work is a comic book entitled *Diary of a Dominatrix.*

Order Form

FOR PLAY

150 Sex Games for Couples

by Walter A. Shelburne, Ph.D.

Send $19.95
+ $4.05 postage and handling to
Waterfall Press
5337 College Avenue, Suite 139
Oakland, CA 94618

Name: _____

Address: _____

City/State/Zip: _____

HumanAwareness Institute

Founded by Stan Dale

The mission of the Human Awareness Institute (HAI) is to empower individuals to know the truth about who they are as potent, loving, contributing human beings. HAI is devoted to promoting personal growth and social evolution by replacing ignorance and fear with awareness and love. The Human Awareness Institute aims to create a world where people live together in dignity, respect, understanding, trust, kindness, honesty and love.

The Human Awareness Institute is committed to creating a world where everyone wins. In support of this mission, the Human Awareness Institute offers a wide variety of workshops, classes and events. These include six levels of the weekend-long Sex, Love & Intimacy Workshops; a day-long workshop on healthy relationships called "Pathways to Intimacy"; and other workshops on Healing Anger, Heart Meditation, Opening to Sexual Intimacy; workshops for businesses called Team Transformations; as well as support groups, parties, meetings and much more. HAI is based in Northern California and offers activities there, as well as around the U.S. and internationally.

These weekend workshops provide you with an opportunity to unfold your infinite capacity to love and be loved. You are supported in discovering and shedding the fears, judgments and disempowering beliefs and behaviors that keep you separate from yourself and others. You are encouraged to explore new ways of relating and communicating that profoundly deepen your ability to be intimate.

Throughout the workshops you significantly improve your relationship with yourself. You uncover your beauty, power and love for self through the simple magic of honesty and authenticity. This increased self-esteem, along with new possibilities for relating, allows you to make exciting and empowering choices in your life and relationships that you never before thought possible. Regardless of your relationship status or sexual preference, the Sex, Love & Intimacy Workshops are for you.

For more information about these workshops or any HAI activities, please call or write to:

Human Awareness Institute
1720 South Amphlett Blvd., Suite 128
San Mateo, CA 94402
415-571-5524 or 800-800-4117

Sensual and Erotic Massage Workshops

for Couples and Friends

One-Day Classes with Don Spencer and staff

Each workshop is a day for you and your partner, along with other couples, to treat yourself to a whole day of body pleasures. Basic massage techniques are demonstrated with attention to those parts usually left out in other classes. We focus on communication and a playful spirit of exploration.

Don is Director of the Massage Institute, and has been teaching and practicing massage since 1973. He has a commitment to supporting and experiencing quality relationships and sensual pleasures.

For class schedules and locations in the San Francisco Bay Area, or to arrange a workshop in your area call:

510-254-3724